BEFORE IT'S BEAUTIFUL

BEFORE IT'S BEAUTIFUL

Every wound had a lesson. Every lesson led me here.

By: Saliya Rose

Before It's Beautiful

Published by Rooted In Her Roses Publishing
Newport News, Virginia

ISBN: 979-8-9950617-0-0

Saliya Rose is a pen name of Ashley Henderson.

Cover design by Saliya Rose

Disclaimer: Names, locations, and identifying details have been altered to protect the privacy of individuals depicted in this work.

Printed in the United States of America

DEDICATION:

To the woman I used to be.
To the woman I am becoming.
To the woman who will rise after her.
You survived.
You bloomed.
You made it here.

Table of Contents

CHAPTER ONE – LOVE IS

All This Love by DeBarge drifts through the living room, floating up to my bedroom on the second floor.

I'm seven years old, lost in Barbie Land, humming along to the music as that feel-good tenderness fills the house. I can smell the meatloaf in the oven, and I just know Momma fixed her buttery, smooth mashed potatoes with it.

My hands are busy working through my doll baby's half matted hair. You know, the doll baby with the bald spot in the middle.

"Saliya!"

Momma's voice cut through the music like a whip, sharp enough to snatch my breath.

My head jerks toward the door on instinct. Panic yanks me to my feet before I even register moving.

The doll slips from my hands and hits the floor with a soft thud, and my feet barely touch the floor as I sprint out of my room.

"Momma! I'm coming!"

But I don't make it.

I stop in the hallway as my body locks in disbelief.

My stomach flips, hot and sick, and my vision blurs with tears.

David's got Momma pinned against the bedroom door, the metal knob scraping the wall so hard that white paint dusts the floor.

One hand clamps tight around her neck. The other presses into her chest.

I watch as David lifts Momma just enough for her black slippers to dangle, toes scraping the floor like she's trying to find the ground again.

When Momma's eyes find mine, they're wide and wild as she claws harder at her neck, fingers slipping against skin, slick with sweat and fear.

"Momma! David, let her go!"

I scream again, louder this time, the words scraping out of my throat until it burns.

My voice bounces off the walls and doesn't feel like mine anymore, but David doesn't even glance at me.

His face twists into something dark, something I've never seen before, like a shadow's taken over him and won't let go.

"Go… get help, Saliya!"

Momma chokes out the words between gasps as she fights for air.

I bolt down the stairs; legs pumping, breath hitching between sobs. The wooden steps sting my bare feet, each one sharper than the last, urging me to move faster.

I don't even realize I'm in just a T-shirt and underwear until the cold, early spring air slaps my skin. The damp grass soaks my toes, the blades clinging to my skin as I run.

I don't stop until my feet hit the pavement; cool and rough as I fly down the street, crying for someone, anyone, to hear me. I see a group of men standing a few houses down. When they see me, they run toward me with protective concern.

I stop and look up, hands on my knees, gasping for air. "He's trying to kill my momma! Please help her!"

One guy scoops me into his arms, following his friends to my house. He smells something like the burning piles of leaves in Grandma's neighborhood, sharp and sweet at the same time.

Everything else is a blur.

Flashing blue lights, shouting, and Momma being pulled out of the house wrapped in a blanket and escorted into her friend Larry's car. Tonight, he's not a friend; he's a savior.

Hmph...Some memories don't fade; they burrow.
They sink into the soft soil of your mind, growing tangled roots you can't dig out—no matter how hard you claw, drink, or cry.
You dodge them like bullets, smiling through the ricochet, pretending your past doesn't still burn.

Maybe beauty is what comes after pain.

CHAPTER TWO – STILL AIR

Grandma's house sits in Pinewood Heights, Smithfield, Virginia, right behind the meat-packing plant. The summer air here is always thick with the smell of pork and metal. The pigs smell like mud and old meat.

The smell hangs in the air like stale cigarette smoke in a closed room, always there, sinking into everything. It even sticks to your clothes and seeps into your hair no matter how long you stay inside.

No, it isn't pleasant, but after a while, you stop noticing.

After us kids get our oatmeal or sweet rice with a side of toast and milk, we're outside chasing the sun. Even when it's hot and heavy, the air pressing against my skin like it wants to smother me, I'm still out there. At 8 years old, it's all I can think about.

This is iceberg weather! That's what I call it. Nothing cools me down like an iceberg from Mrs. Georgia's house up the road. Purple's my favorite.

She serves them in Styrofoam cups, the crushed ice crunching between my teeth before it melts into something syrupy and sweet that slides down my throat.

Our feet can't move fast enough, running up and down the dirt hill out back, the one with the pond at the bottom, hiding behind trees like secrets. I know I'm not supposed to be here, but we still sneak down. We poke at sand fiddler crabs until they pinch our fingers, and we toss them back into the water, squealing.

We race our bikes up and down the paved hill beside it, wind burning our cheeks, laughing so hard we almost tip over.

Behind Grandma's house, the brush sways in the breeze. If you run your hand across the tall grass, its feather-soft tops will tickle your palms. When the sun starts dipping low, bikes drop, and the smell of charcoal takes over the neighborhood.

That's when the family packs into Auntie's yard for cookouts, just a few houses down from Grandma's. The air smells like charcoal and grilled chicken, and the grown folks lean back in lawn chairs with their cans of beer, laughing loud enough to spill into the street.

Momma has the best cartwheel I've ever seen, landing with her hair wild and her laugh even wilder. Sometimes those cookouts run so late the grown folks forget to tell us no, and that's when the sleepovers happen.

We stay up all night building pillow forts, whispering until we fall asleep in a heap. The best part? Waking up to Aunt Stephanie's crispy bacon popping in the pan. The smell pulls me from my sleep and into the kitchen, with cheese eggs made just the way I like them.

I want to stay here forever.

"Don't get too close to the road, Saliya!"

Grandma calls out to me, slicing through my memories from the day before.

I look over and catch her rubbing her feet together in her white plastic yard chair, the way she always does when she's at ease. She has on her long white dress with the roses to match her gigantic rose bush at the side of her house.

Not even looking up, I try to carry my voice so she can hear me. "Yes, ma'am!"

I look over and see her pink house shoes, looks like she's had them since I was born. The slippers are sitting at the foot of the chair, the dusty imprint of her heels worn deep into the fabric.

Grandma's right back to laughing on the phone, her voice warm.

For a moment, everything is still; it's perfect. But then there's a shift...

I freeze mid-jump, my rope hits the dirt, and I grab my stomach. "Where did everyone go? Grandma?!"

I don't hear the neighbors, the birds, and I don't feel a breeze.

The sun is gone.

I look up, squinting my eyes to make sense of the dark clouds I see spinning in the sky.

"Grandma!!" Louder this time, but I don't hear her.

I don't even see her. Maybe my eyes are playing tricks on me.

Tears blur my vision. My breath turns sharp and shallow; the air muffles in my ears like they're about to pop as the wind suddenly picks up, but I can't catch it.

Then it hits, a deafening roar that shakes the ground. One thought takes over:
RUN NOW, SALIYA. It's a tornado.

One minute I'm jumping rope. Next, I'm running for my life. Each step makes the ground stretch even further.

This time, the wind doesn't just roar. The funnel tears through everything in its path: my jump rope, my grandmother's rose bush, even the sound of her laughter.

And still I run, feet sinking into the dirt like quicksand.

The wind grabs me before I can make it to the cellar door, yanking with a strength I can't fight. Somewhere far away, my momma's voice screams my name, but it's far away now.

My body goes limp.

CHAPTER THREE – A SUMMER DAZE

I wake up gasping, mid-scream, clutching my chest. Sweat slicks my skin, my bonnet's halfway off, my socks gone.

"Saliya! Aye! You gonna lay up in that bed all day?"

Momma's voice breaks through the walls from the kitchen. It's that tone, the one that makes your nerves stand at attention and never misses its mark.

I roll my eyes, stretching, still halfway stuck in the tail end of the tornado dream. My skin is sticky, and my locs are plastered to my forehead.

"Damn, can I wake up first?" I say, mumbling under my breath.

Momma appears in the doorway, coffee in hand like it holds all the wisdom she swears I don't have. With one hand on her hip, she drills holes clean through me with her eyes.

"Look, Saliya! Watch your mouth. And don't 'damn' me when you sittin' in my house, in my AC, eating my food!"

My eyes follow her as she walks to the window and snatches my curtains open.

I suck my teeth and swing my legs off the bed, my toes brushing the wood floor that always creaks in protest.

"I'm trying to figure things out, Momma. Marcus only has a few months left till he's backkk." I sing it out in that sarcastic tone she hates, wiping the sweat dripping down my temple.

She cut her eyes, turning back toward the kitchen.

It's summer 2003, and I thought I had freedom all figured out when I ran off and married Marcus last December. It was one week after I turned 18 years old. I thought marrying him would be my ticket out, but this sure as hell isn't the fairytale I pictured.

He's at Fort Jackson for basic training, shipped out for the Army one month after we got married.

I admired his strength when we met in high school. He carried responsibility like armor, and back then, that looked like safety to me.

Me? I'm right back at Momma's house sweating through another hot-ass summer in Newsome Park Apartments. Momma moved us here July 1995, and this has been home ever since.

Newsome Park Apartments isn't what folks call the best neighborhood, but it's home. Brick buildings line the block, and the hard tile floors stay cold no matter how high you turned the heat. Momma had carpet laid down, though; a burgundy, green, beige mix she picked herself.

"Saliya, you been 'figuring' since you landed back here in January. I don't know why y'all ran off and got married so fast. That sure was stupid!"

My eyes narrow, "Momma...it's too early."

"Too early? Or are you just late...Anyway, Saliya, when are you gonna *do* something with yourself, little girl?"

I let out a hard sigh.

"Soon, Momma. Soon. Okay? Can you turn on some air boo?"

"Can you pay the electric bill, Saliya?"

"I love you too, Momma!"

She glances over her shoulder; eyebrows raised; lips pressed so tight you would've thought she bit into a lemon.

"Mmm hmm. 'Soon.' You sound just like your daddy. Everything coming soon and never showing up at the same damn time."

What can I even say to that? Because… where has he been?

My father's been a ghost in plain sight my whole life. Around just enough to remind me of what I was missing, gone just enough to keep my heart confused about what I was longing for.

I might as well file "Daddy" under "desolate" in my personal dictionary.

To Momma's credit, she never forced me to chase after him. She let me decide. And I respect her for that.

Momma disappears back toward the kitchen, and the room settles…. until the cordless phone rings.

"Hello?" I say, my voice still carrying leftover frustration.

"Saliya, sweetie!"

My body jerks upright, tense, and my eyes widen.

"Marcus?! When are you coming back?" Hearing his voice yanks me back through time. Shit, I almost forgot I was married.

But the truth is, I wasn't running toward Marcus as much as I was running away from Momma. She tried so hard to protect me from the world as I got older. Her grip was so tight, it ended up pushing me straight into the next chapter of my life.

Momma? Oh, she had my things packed by the time I got back home from the courthouse; "Get out right now."

And so, I did...

Marriage. Army wife. Grown-up, on paper. Child in spirit.

And here we are...

"...But that's all I know right now, okay? Saliya!? I said I'll be back around mid-August. SALIYA!! Do you hear me?!?"

"Oh, okay, Marcus, can't wait to see you!" I blink as my head jolts back to the conversation.

Hearing his excited tone catches me off guard, drowning out my thoughts.

"But, sweetheart, I had to call and let you know we're being stationed at Fort Sill. That's in Oklahoma."

I gurgle and then cough as a little water slides down my throat. "Oklahoma?" My glass slams onto the dresser.

"Marcus, you sure? Because let's be real… haven't I been predicting my death with these tornado dreams for years? So, basically, I'm about to die…"

"Saliya, I promise we will be fine. It's a new adventure."

I swallow hard and stretch my face into a smile he can't even see. I try to match his energy, try to sound like the wife who believes in her husband… who believes in our future. "Well, babe, okay. You know what, that's great, and I can't wait!"

My voice jumps to this high, playful pitch I don't even recognize. It's survival mode, because deep down I feel like I'm about to die.

"And I hope your ass ain't been dressing crazy out there while I'm away, Saliya. I told you to throw all that skimpy shit away. If I don't like it, you're throwing it out." He follows up with that obnoxious laugh.

Just like that, Marcus reminds me that my choices aren't really mine. Control isn't mine. From Momma's house to my husband's house, I just keep trading cages.

I laugh too, but mine is hollow, the sound pulled tight around fear. Anxiety claws at me, whispering that maybe I rushed into this marriage. Maybe I wasn't finished being...me.

"Of course, Marcus, I'm not dressing crazy, but I'll go through my clothes again. You know, just to be sure." I say, forcing sweetness into my voice while my face betrays me with silent disdain.

"I love you to pieces!"

I hang on to that fake excitement, even as tension wraps me like barbed wire, we end the call.

The phone slips from my hand onto the bed, and I press my palm to my face, accepting my fate.

I drag myself toward the shower with a long face and racing mind.

"What kind of weird coincidence is this, Lord?" I say to myself, mind churning. I need to get dressed, get out, and let the air hit my face.

Plus, Momma needs space to unclench; she stays so tense, and it's unbearable today.

When I step out of the shower, I wipe the steam off the mirror. I catch my reflection and smile at the scar under my eye.

It's become my badge of honor, in a funny way. A tiny reminder of how clumsy I have always been, even before I hit kindergarten.

I slipped off the metal pail Momma had me standing on while she did my hair and smacked my face on the toilet bowl. Next thing I remember, I was in the hospital bed, getting stitches.

This scar has been my hilarious stamp ever since. Everyone loves to ask about it, and I love to avoid telling the story.

I used to think that was the only scar that mattered. Turns out, I've collected a few more since then, not the kind you can cover with makeup, either.

Life has a way of handing them out when you're just trying to love and survive at the same time.

CHAPTER FOUR – DON'T TELL ME YOUR NAME

When I step outside, sweat beads up on my forehead before I hit the sidewalk, reminding me it's June on the coast of Virginia. I press my lips together, reaching for my facecloth.

"Ugh, humid again."

As I bring the cloth to my forehead, I see him.
Him, as in… Jacoby.

His skin is that light brown that glows in the sun, eyes a shade lighter, hair sandy and curly, like he doesn't even try and still wins. Slim build, clothes fitting just right.

For a second, I allow myself to admire him, standing there like he don't care about a single thing except himself. So fine that it actually pisses me off a little bit.

Every time I cross his path, we linger a little too long. Long enough for me to know this man is on a mission.

"Hmph."
I exhale and pretend to be unimpressed, picking

up my pace to avoid the temptation. But for a split second, his eyes lock on mine.

Saliya, girl, don't look at him!

I try to find a quick detour around him, but it's too late. He smirks, and I can't turn away as he lifts his chin and nods.

"Aye, Chocolate, come here real quick."

I flinch because his voice hits me before I can avoid crossing his path, and I roll my eyes. I look left, then right, and then look at him.

"Jacoby, what do you want? You know I'm very much married."

My voice comes out tired, even as my heart hammers against my chest. It's one last effort to push him away before I give in and, truth be told, I want to.

After the conversation I just had, I'm trying to figure out why I even got married?

"It's all respect, beautiful," Jacoby says as he walks toward me. His voice is low, the kind that makes you forget your own name and sends a silent tremor down your spine.

"I just figured you could use a friend. Baby girl you look real damn lonely out here."

A nervous laugh slips out as I twist the damp facecloth in my hand, trying to wring out the tension crawling up my arms.

Then, I get a whiff of his cologne.

Oh, my goodness.

I spin away to hide the smile tugging at my lips because I want to melt.

"Yeah, whatever, Jacoby. I got enough friends."

I toss the cloth in the air with a wave, strutting off in the opposite direction before he can see how much I'm lying.

"Don't you wanna ride with me to run some errands?"

His voice softens for me, like he already knows what my answer should be.

I hesitate just long enough to cling to what dignity I have left, then turn back toward him.

"And how do I know you're not a murderer or a stalker? Some kind of crazy person? I don't even know your damn last name."

I narrow my eyes at him.

"It's—"

I throw up a hand, cutting him off before he can finish.

"Nope! Don't tell me; I don't wanna know your full name." If this man tells me his name, I'll be too invested. I'm gonna start stalking him or some shit.

"Well, I'm not crazy, I promise. Why would I wanna hurt something that looks so damn good, huh?" he says.

"Oh boy, save the pickup line, please. That was awful. You shouldn't even be talking to me, but you're so damn persistent."

I scrunch up my face but, mmm, that was very impressive.

"Well, shit, guess I'm gonna die smiling then, just you talking to me right now," he says.

Okay, cute, but I am fighting for my life to keep my composure.

"Anyway, Jacobyyy," I cave in 5...4...3...2...

"I was going to the store, but I guess that can wait. Let me grab my bag. You are something else."

I don't give myself time to feel shame.

"Oh, shit, you for real?" he says, "Your fine chocolate self. Imma pull the car around front." And just like that, he strolls off.

My eyes follow his frame; I'm 5'5" and he's just a little taller than me. White t-shirt clinging to his back, blue jean shorts hanging just right, down to his shoes. Mmm, and he smells so damn good. Nice walk, too.

Lord, keep me from myself, because I don't want to fold.

I try to scold myself, but it doesn't stick.

Outside, the wind picks up, rattling the thin apartment windows. I don't notice it yet; I'm too hyped, already looking forward to hopping in this man's car.

Inside the apartment, I tie a bandana over my head, half-finished box braids swinging down my back, and grab my purse.

The walls begin to thump with Lil Jon and the East Side Boyz, and I just know it's Jacoby pulling in the parking lot. The bass rattles my chest as I cut through the kitchen and head straight to the front door.

My stepdad steps away from the fridge, blocking my path, eyes tight and focused.

"Look, Saliya, whatever this is, you keep it outside my house."

His scowl pisses me off, low enough so Momma doesn't hear. He glances once more before sliding into the living room.

"Whatever. Don't act like you care now."

My face twists with disgust at the attempt to check me as the storm door slams shut behind me.

Jacoby's black Expedition rounds the corner, sunlight dancing on the fresh black paint. He slows just enough for me to hop in, one hand loose on the wheel, the other resting on his thigh, never even putting the car in park.
He looks me over, licking his lips.

"Damn, you ain't waste no time, huh?"
That 'up-to-no-good' smirk spreads across my face as I slide the seat back, getting comfortable.

"Well, neither did you."

I laugh and lean my head back as I allow the moment to wash over me. I feeling freer than my conscience should ever allow as Jacoby rests his hand on my knee. For a second, I forget everything.

Then it hits, the guilt, like ice in my veins.

Marcus.

My voice screams at me, but I push it down.

Over the next few months, Jacoby is a distraction. A dangerous, beautiful distraction. Taking me away from everything that was bothering me.

He has a way of pulling me into his world, holding me hostage all day, and making me forget about right and wrong. The danger isn't in his charm; it's in how easy it is to lose myself around him. With him, there are no rules, no boundaries.

He makes me feel invincible, even though I know we're doing something risky, something wrong. For a moment while we are together, I forget that I'm in a marriage I don't want to be in.

The worst part? He knows Marcus. Everyone around us knows Marcus. I cringe at the thought, but I just can't say no; it hurts too good.

We live in the moment every day, from sunrise to sunset. It's our world. But I know it has to end soon.

"Let's do something different tonight," Jacoby says one evening, his hand resting on the gearshift.

"Not just riding around here, same old shit. Let's go somewhere we can really be ourselves."

"Like what?" I tease, even though I already like where his mind is going.

His lips curl into a grin.

"Musiq Soulchild. 9:30 Club. We're driving to D.C. tonight."

I laugh, shaking my head. "You're crazy."

"Nah, I'm serious." He leans over and whispers, like it's a secret meant just for me. "You deserve something different, Saliya. Come on, let's go."

A few hours later, we're shoulder to shoulder in the crowded 9:30 Club, sweat and perfume swirling together under the dim lights. The stage glows blue, and the bass of *"Love"* vibrates through the walls. Jacoby pulls me close, his palm steady on my back, anchoring me in the music.

We move slowly, swaying with the crowd, his forehead pressed to mine.

"You feel that?" he murmurs against my ear.

"Yeah," I whisper back as I close my eyes and sink into the warmth of his presence, his grip.

For this moment, it's just us.

But then my eyes lift over his shoulder, scanning the crowd without meaning to, and my stomach drops.

A familiar face. Marcus' cousin.

She's laughing with her boyfriend, head turned toward the stage, not looking at me, yet. My body tenses like a wire about to snap.

I grip Jacoby's shirt.

"Don't look now, but Marcus' cousin is here."

His hand tightens at my waist, his eyes flickering with annoyance.

"Where?"

"Back by the bar. She hasn't seen me, but..."

I can't even finish the thought.

"Come on," he says, guiding me through the crowd, cutting past clusters of swaying bodies.

We find a darker corner near the back of the venue, the music still wrapping around us, but I'm sick with anxiousness.

"Relax, baby," Jacoby murmurs, brushing his lips against my temple.

"Ain't nobody worried about her."

"But I am! What if she sees me and says something. Oh my god. What am I doing?"

I grab his arm tighter and he pulls me closer.

"Look, ain't nothing to worry about long as you're with me. I'm not gonna let anybody near you. Even if he finds out about us and shit goes down… fuck him, can't do shit to either of us, Saliya!"

His words are equal parts fire and gasoline.

While one side of me cringes at the recklessness, another side shivers at the way he says *mine* without saying it. An intimate relationship with danger and love just brewing without me knowing it.

Musiq shifts into another slow groove, and Jacoby sings in my ear, soft, off-key, his breath warm against my neck.

But the tension won't leave. It sits between us like a shadow we can't shake. We sway, pretending to enjoy the show, pretending I'm not terrified of being caught, pretending I don't feel eyes crawling across the room toward me.

Later that night at the hotel, the mood is quieter, gentler. Jacoby just lies beside me, thumb stroking the back of my hand, as if holding me is enough. It's not enough to stop the inevitable.

CHAPTER FIVE – THE HARD GOODBYE

It's August 7ᵗʰ, and I know Marcus will be home tomorrow. At Jacoby's cousin's empty apartment in Hampton, our first stop of the last day, he pulls me close, his eyes tracing my skin like he's memorizing me.

"You are so damn beautiful," he says as his hand caresses my cheek, "where'd this scar come from? What happened?"

"Don't ask; it's embarrassing," I say, holding back a laugh.

"Nah, you gotta tell me now, Saliya. Come on."

"Fine," I sigh. "When I was little, I hit my head on the toilet bowl. Bled everywhere. Stitches. Real glamorous origin story."

Jacoby's eyes widen, "DAMN! I know that shit knocked you out."

I turn my head with a straight face. "I mean, I don't remember much about it, so maybe so. Childhood was wild."

We both laugh as he pulls me into his chest.

"I wasn't expecting all this, all these feelings and shit, why you do me like this."

"Eh, just being myself, love, just being myself."

"Look, Saliya, I want you to come with me; leave him. I'm moving to Alexandria."

His breath warms my ear, sending shivers down my spine, and my heart flutters.

"Jacoby, you know I can't."

He stops me before I can finish...

"Come here. Gimme a kiss, girl."

"Oh... okay." The words slide out before he tilts my chin up and kisses me.

We melt into the couch, locking together like puzzle pieces. A tear falls from my eye because I know I'm breaking a vow; I can see Marcus's face, sadness written all over it. But I come back to reality, what's in front of me.

Jacoby.

Jacoby is gentle but purposeful, soothing my rough spots like he means every movement.

I've never experienced real love or an orgasm, but he still satisfies me.

For the rest of the day, we relax at his sister's place in Hampton. We're in the sun playing with her dogs, and it feels like we're a thriving, loving couple.

"You know it's our last day together, Jacoby."

I pet the dog with one hand while sliding my shoes on with the other.

He doesn't say a word, just grabs his keys and walks out the door to the car. I shuffle behind him, sharing an uncomfortable smile with his sister as we wave goodbye to one another.

In the car, Jacoby breaks the silence swallowing us.
"Aiight."

He exhales, "Imma take you back home now."

"Okay," I say, frustration slipping into my voice. Not frustration with him, but with the situation.

The radio plays I'll Never Leave by R. Kelly, and the lyrics feel like a promise.

I stare out the window, biting the inside of my cheek.

Who am I? What do I want and what am I even doing?

Jacoby glances over at me, placing a hand on my thigh.

"So… are you still going to Oklahoma?"

"Yeah… I mean, he is my husband, so I have to, right?"

All I can do is pick at the hem of my dress and continue to avoid eye contact, face hot. He doesn't respond right away. His jaw flexes, eyes locked on the road.

"Damn shame," he says, almost like he's talking to himself.

I look at him, and my heart folds in on itself. I don't know how to feel because we spent the summer wrapped up in each other, and I can't see not doing this. With him, not Marcus. I'm delusional, and I don't care. Just give me my little clown shoes and red nose, dammit.

"Jacoby, I'll tell him I want a divorce."

I peel at my chipped purple nail polish, trying to act casual, like I'm not breaking my heart.

He stares off, looks like he's deciding whether to hold on or let go, but we both know this is the end.

When Jacoby drops me off for the last time, the gravel crunches under his tires, mourning with me. He glances back once, and that's enough. A single tear slips down my cheek. Then he's gone, and I promise myself at that moment that I'll never stop trying to find my way back to him.

The emptiness feels bigger than the goodbye. It aches, not for Jacoby, but for the girl I had just started to discover. This summer showed me all my unfinished parts; raw, jagged, still aching.

As I fall back onto my pillow, the regret and pain transforms into something familiar as I close my eyes.

Suddenly, I'm fifteen again, pure happiness in my heart.

My friend Val's inviting me to house-sit with her at her godmother's place, two doors down, and so we walk there...the wind picks up.

The sky darkens. Somewhere in the distance and I hear the low growl of a storm getting closer. There's laughter as we sneak liquor from the cabinet; cheap, bitter, and burning down my throat. My head spins as the doorbell rings.

The sirens wail and the house shudders. My heart skips a beat.

They come in. Next thing I know, I'm downstairs, on the couch, with a stranger I don't even know. But I know what he wants, and I can feel myself shifting, trying to escape, but I can't. I say no, but he doesn't care.

The tornado roars in the background, tearing through the walls. My words scatter, shredded by the wind before they can leave my mouth.

He pulls at me, rough, unrelenting; my voice doesn't exist. I sit frozen, too afraid to scream, too afraid to make my "no" heard. Tears run down while the storm swallows the sound.

The funnel twists tighter. My body aches. I look past him, and the air is ripped from my lungs as I see a storm cellar in the distance.

As the moment passes, I slip a dress over my skin, thin fabric covering a silence that already feels permanent.

Is there pleasure without brutal fucking pain?

The words repeat over and over in my head. It's planted something inside me. Rotten, growing, choking out everything else.

It whispers that my voice doesn't matter, and that no one will hear me scream for help.

Grabbing my bag with my clothes, all I can do is run, but the storm keeps circling me. I still don't trust it.

I see Jacoby's car in the distance.

I chase him, but he continues to drive away further, further...

The sky breaks wide open.

The funnel touches down. Debris spins around me, Jacoby's smile, Marcus's shadow and his devious smile, the pieces of me I'll never get back.

I open my mouth to scream. Nothing comes out.

The tornado takes it. It takes my innocence; it takes my voice.

And then, I wake up.

Soaked in sweat, chest tight, tears dried on my cheeks.

The silence is still there, pressing down, heavier than the dream I just woke up from.

I sit still, clutching at my throat and trying to catch my breath.

Am I fifteen again? Nineteen? I don't know because all sense of reality blurs in these damn dreams. I'm so sick of it.

And then I hear a knock at the door…

Well, Marcus is back.

"Marcus, I can't do this. I don't want to be married anymore. I'm sorry."

The words fall out before I can rehearse them. They're soft, but solid. I stare at the worn carpet on Momma's apartment floor, praying the shit will swallow me whole.

His breathing changes and his body stiffens, sending fear through my chest as I glance up at him, still in uniform.

"We're not gettin' a divorce."

His voice is cold, his fist clenched like he's holding back more than words.

"Get your stuff. We leave for Oklahoma in a few days."

That's it. No talk. No questions. A verdict, and I have to comply.

The last thing I want is to stay married to this man while I'm in love with another man, but here we go.

CHAPTER SIX – FAIRYTALES DON'T COME TRUE

It's time.

I grab my things and toss them into the car, silent, numb. I haven't said a word about the Jacoby, but something tells me he knows, or at least suspects. The guilt is so loud in my body; it feels like it's bouncing off the windows.

The next morning, we stop by Momma's, saying goodbye before the long 24-hour drive to Oklahoma. She's standing at the curb, crying. I'm crying too, but not for the reason either of them thinks.

These aren't happy tears; I'm crying because I'm leaving my life behind, the one I wish was mine. Not the one sitting next to me, driving me away from everything that feels like freedom.

Everything disappears in the rearview as Marcus and I push through an excruciating two-day drive.

When we finally pull up to the base hotel, the atmosphere feels lighter. We'll be staying until we find housing off base.

I should feel broken, defeated even, but a stubborn flicker of hope burns inside me.

A fresh start. A different place.

I'm a wife.

I crack a slight smile at the thought.

I grab my journal from the front seat and walk inside.

Marcus has already unloaded most of the things we'll need over the next few weeks, so I join him, setting my journal on top of the dresser. When we're done, I sink into the king-size bed, memory foam wrapping around my back like a hug.

I pull off my socks and wiggle my toes.

Okay, Saliya... we're here. Girl, let's make the best of it. You're happy; you're fucking ecstatic.

As we settle in for the evening and Marcus's breathing slips into the heavy rhythm of snores, I lay staring at the ceiling, wide awake.

The blanket feels heavier than usual, pressing me into the mattress. My thoughts drift, as they always seem to, back to Jacoby; the heat of that summer, the laughter, the way just thinking of him could send a little electricity dancing across my skin.

Almost without realizing it, my hand slides lower, resting against myself in a way I had never dared. A flicker of curiosity sparks, and I hesitate, holding my breath. But then... something stirs. My breathing quickens, shallow and uneven. *What is this?* The feeling is unfamiliar, but it's hard to ignore.

So I stay with it, following the pulse, letting my fingers move with a new boldness. The more I lean into it, the more my body answers back. It's an intensity building, curling tighter and tighter until suddenly, it breaks open like a wave crashing over me.

My body trembles, and I bite my lip, muffling the sound that almost escapes.

Marcus is inches away, dead to the world, and here I am... discovering something he had never given me, not once!

I lay still in shock, chest heaving, staring into the dark. As Tweet's song, Oops, plays in my head, a quiet laugh slips out before I can stop it.

"Well, shit," I whisper to myself, "that's never happened before."

I drift off into the most peaceful sleep, thinking about Jacoby.

It's the first week in October when we are finally able to move from the temporary housing on base to our own house off base.

As Marcus and I settle in for the night, the quiet between us is unusual. Not peaceful; it's brittle, full of the things we both know but refuse to say.

Dinner is a disaster, and I'm disappointed because it's my first home-cooked meal. The chicken is dry, the mashed potatoes thick and salty as hell, but he doesn't say a word. Neither do I.

"Saliya, thanks for dinner. I'm hitting the road in the morning to get the rest of our things. I'm leaving you the car, but don't even think about going outside unless you have to. Unless it's an emergency.

I'll fly out, grab the moving truck, and drive back. I'll be home next Wednesday."

I lean over and press a quick kiss to his lips.

"Okay, babe."

He lifts his cup for a sip and sets it on the plastic bin doubling as our nightstand.

"Let's read the Bible together before we go to sleep."

I blink, lowering onto my side of the blow-up mattress, feeling sick to my stomach. Did I hear that right?

"I guess, sure, we could do that. Where did this come from?"

He reaches for the bible.

"Let god lead me, and I lead you, right?"

My eyebrows furrow because there seems to be an underlying motive.

"Hmm, okay...Marcus."

This has never been something in our routine. Not once.

Marcus flips the Bible open like he's pulling a card from a shuffled deck. No searching, no hesitation. He lands on a page and starts reading.

"Hebrews 13:4."

His voice is firm and his eyes shift between me and the words.

"Marriage should be honored by all, and the marriage bed kept pure, for God will judge the adulterer and all the sexually immoral."

He closes the Bible slowly and sets it down on the makeshift nightstand. Then his gaze meets mine. The silence is suffocating.

"Wow," He says, followed up with a devious laugh, "I randomly opened to that page. What a coincidence, right?"

There's a curl to his lips, something between amusement and accusation, which makes my stomach churn.

Still, I laugh through the uncomfortable silence that settles in the room.

I glance at him as I reach for my glass of water, breaking eye contact to calm my nerves.

"What a coincidence? Feels like the opening to a scary ass movie to me, Marcus. Very odd start to couple's bible study, don't you think?"

"Oh, so you think that's funny?"

Well, shit, I thought it was hilarious. I guess he doesn't like my joke.

"Huh? Mann... whew, my throat is so dry."

I can feel his stare burning through me as I reach for my glass.

Shit. He knows.

Marcus leaves the next morning, and I'm left in the house alone.

It's just me smelling this musty-ass, ugly blue carpet. Arrest whoever put this down; it's so ugly. It looks like they killed Grover and laid him out in my house.

"Why does it smell like this in here?"

I scrunch my face, holding down the cheeseburger I just ate.

"Is it the walls? The carpet? The chicken from last night? Did something die in here?"

I'm overcome by the nausea I've been trying to ignore; it's too much now.

And then it hits me…

"When is my period supposed to come?"

I spin in a circle like the answer is going to fall from the ceiling into my ditsy brain.

I don't even have a license yet, just a learner's permit, but desperation is louder than fear today. Marcus left the car and the keys with me strictly for emergencies only.

"Well, this is an emergency!" I shout, and the empty house throws my words right back at me.

I grab the keys and step outside.

The sky is heavy, bruised, swollen like it's holding back a breakdown.
Okay, Saliya… You won't die today; it's just a storm. You're gonna be okay.

I follow the directions Marcus drilled into me before he left, hands tight on the wheel, sweaty palms. I make it to the drugstore just as the rain decides to up its wages.

Sheets of water slam against the windshield like they're trying to get in.

When I step out, the air is electric, restless. The clouds above me start twisting slowly, like they're thinking about spinning themselves into something dangerous.

My nerves kick in and my heartbeat is everywhere, my chest, my throat, my ears.

Inside the store, thunder rolls so loud it rattles the shelves. I grab the pregnancy tests with shaking hands and head straight to the register, praying the cashier can't see the panic sitting on my skin.

As soon as the automatic doors open, all hell breaks loose.

Wind whips sideways.

Debris fly.

Something metal clatters across the parking lot like it's running for its life.

A tornado, *it has to be a tornado.*

I don't have a cell phone. I don't have anyone to call or a way to call them. All I have is a learner's permit, a car I'm barely allowed to drive, and a storm that feels like it's hunting me.

I sprint to the car and jump in, breathing out in little bursts. Visibility is trash; I can't see in front of me, behind me, or inside myself. I just drive. Instinct takes over.

The wind screams. Sirens start wailing in the distance; long, hollow, that bone-deep warning sound that makes your soul sit up straight.

Lord... I want my momma.

But the closer I get to our street, the more something primal kicks in. My body is in full survival mode. Shaking, alert, pushing the car faster even though I can't see clearly. The sirens are louder now, echoing off the houses.

I turn the corner onto our block. The car jumps the curb and slams to a stop in front of the house, but I don't care; I'm out, already running.

Inside. Lock the door. Bathroom. No windows.
I drop to my knees and pray through my tears until the thunder quiets, and the sirens die away.

No tornado... not today. Just a warning.

A warning I'll never forget.

I damn near tear the box open. I snatch out the test, the paper, all of it.

My body is still rattling from my first drive alone, and my mind is racing. My heart pounds, and I pause for a moment.

If I don't move, maybe this moment won't be real.

I close my eyes and hang my head, resting on the toilet, pants at my ankles.

I can't be pregnant... or... could I?

A smile spreads across my face, like my body's trying to lie to me. But just like that, it flips.

The smile slides off my face, and I'm crying before I even know what's happening. Ugly crying too. The kind that makes your nose burn.

"This just can't be happening right now...Jacoby?"

I rock like somebody's grandma at a prayer altar and then I look down at the stick.

"What the fuck."

Two pink lines.

I grab the trash can and throw up everything, which pisses me off even more because my cheeseburger was delicious.

My body gives out, knees folding like a busted chair, forcing me back onto the toilet.

I press my palms to my eyes in an attempt to squeeze the moment out of existence, but it doesn't work.

Relief washes over me as I realize the timeline doesn't match the moment Jacoby and I were last together. It's been months.

I slide off the toilet and onto the cold tile floor, pants still at my ankles.

"Okay. Dumbass. You're going to be fine. Relax."

Excitement replaces my nervousness, washing over me with relief. I scramble for the house phone to call Marcus.

"Marcus?" My breath and my words are out of sync. "I'm pregnant."

To my surprise, he's excited to hear the news. He doesn't ask any questions, and I don't cause a bigger scene. I still don't know what he knows, if he knows, or if I want him to know what happened over the summer.

We just...take in the moment.

CHAPTER SEVEN – A PERFECT FAMILY PICTURE

A few days later, Marcus is back, and he has this pep in his step. I know I have to push through, try to make the best of an uncomfortable situation. I mean, we're having a baby.

He sits the first load of our things down on the living room floor and kisses my cheek. I give him space as he gets straight to work setting up our new life before reporting to work in one week.

It's official, we're in "adulting" mode, and I land my first job at a bank on the military base.

"Hi, Saliya. We're glad to have you here at Members First Federal Credit Union," my new manager says. Her voice is warm with a sound of optimism that's comforting.

"I know you mentioned you're pregnant. There's someone I want you to meet!"

"Yayyyyy..." I drag the word out with furrowed brows, trying to cover the fact that my introvert self is already bracing for awkward small talk.

She waves someone over. A woman approaches, a little hesitant at first, but with a glow that fills the room. She's short with gorgeous caramel brown skin, and her hair, in a natural puff, sits on top of her head. She looks like she's my age.

"Saliya, this is Marie. Marie, this is Saliya. You're both pregnant!"

Marie's face lights up. "Oh my God, no way!" she bursts out, and we laugh like we've just shared an inside joke.

We step in for a hug, natural, like we've been friends forever and just didn't know it until now.

The next six months fly by, and it's April 2004. I realize Marie is the lifeline I didn't know I needed. She makes being away from home feel a little more normal, and it's ironic that our due dates are both in May: hers, May 24th; mine, May 2nd.

We waddle through work like two overstuffed penguins, side by side, swollen ankles and all. Sharing cravings, aversions, swapping stretch mark oil, and comparing baby names.

We spend more time together than we do with our own husbands. We're both 19-year-old wives, and we bask in late-night talks, belly laughs, church services, even hair-washing experiments become our life.

"Let's do it," I say. You'd think we're about to rob a bank, not just wash hair.

"Bad idea, girl, bad idea," she says, leaning over the sink as water drips down her arms and stomach.

We both figure it's a good idea because the sink is high and neither of us can even tie our shoes.

She huffs and laughs as we switch places and now she's struggling to rinse my conditioner out.

"Saliya! I told you! Girl, these bellies are so damn big, I can't reach nothin'! Hey, what happened to your face right here?" She says, as she sprays leave in conditioner in my hair.

"Fell when I was 4, head hit the toilet, blood, stitches."

"DAMN! Glad you still got your eye."

"Yes, yes, girl, me too." I say as I roll my eyes. "You know how many times I tell that story? A LOT!"

"Well, I'm gonna just call you Mary J Blige."

We both laugh, soaking wet, ridiculous, and completely at ease. She's already my sister.

Marie is the friend every woman needs, but only a few are lucky enough to have. Standing about 5'3", she's slim like me, except for these bellies, and she has this magnetic energy that fills any room she walks into.

Her style is effortlessly bold, always rocking oversized hoop doorknocker earrings, fresh nails, and a perfectly natural slicked bun or a carefree twist-out, depending on the mood.

Her laugh is deep and contagious, the kind that makes other people laugh even if they don't know what's funny.

But Marie isn't only style and sass, she's substance. She has a sharp tongue, a sharper mind, and a heart that holds space for people, especially me.

She's the one who shows up with wine when I feel like the world is falling apart. The one who listens without judgment but won't let me drown in my self-pity either. She curses me with love, tells the truth even if it's painful, and always encourages me.

She won't back down.

Her loyalty? Unmatched. Her love? Unshakable.

As fate would have it, Marie goes into labor on May 8th, 2004, and I'm still here, miserably, pregnant as hell.

She's in the hospital, feet up, probably eating ice chips. Meanwhile, I'm Googling "how to evict a baby."

I land on castor oil, and it seems harmless enough. One spoonful down, and it's disgusting, but we've got action.

I'm in labor a few hours later, rocking and crying on an exercise ball, don't know if I have to pee or poop.

By midnight, I can't take it anymore.

I grunt through a painful contraction, and I try to get Marcus' attention. "Marcus. Marcus, I think we need to go to the hospital."

"Okay, sweetie… set an alarm for 5am; let's see how you're feeling," he mumbles through his snore, so unbothered it's criminal.

I cut my eyes at him so hard I almost birthed the baby with the look alone.

I grit my teeth through another contraction. "Okay, babe."

Spoiler alert: 5am ain't happening. By 2am, we're speeding to the hospital like *The Fast and the Fertile.*

Finally, on May 10th, 2004, my baby girl Nicole makes her grand entrance. Two days apart. Marie's son and my daughter. A matched set, born into chaos and love.

This friendship is heaven sent.

By April 2005, Marcus and I do the best we can to look like we've got it together.

He's out of the military now, medically discharged because his foot never healed right after breaking it last year. He lands a job managing the local McDonald's. Decent money. Steady hours. I don't complain. I can't complain.

On paper, we look stable. Smiling. Bills paid. Baby fed. But that's the surface. Just the surface. Underneath it all, I suffer behind closed doors while Marcus keeps me locked away in plain sight.

He controls everything about my existence, and I can feel myself unraveling, one day at a time.

I don't leave the house without him, and if I do, I have to be very mindful of how long I'm gone. I have to use the house phone, no cell phone, and I only have one friend, Marie. He doesn't even like me going to church too much without him.

No matter how loud I sing on Sundays, no matter how hard I press my face into the altar carpet, there's no prayer loud enough to erase how lost I feel inside.

Then, the rough gets rougher… fast.

We're in bed. Not talking. Not fighting. Just… existing next to each other like two strangers who share a rent payment. Marcus sits up and turns to me slowly.

"Saliya ... I quit my job today," he says, calm as if he's announcing dinner.

So casual that it's offensive, and he stares straight at me, waiting for a reaction. I blink, my mouth tight. "Huh?"

That's all I can get out. I keep trying to move my mouth more, but my brain is struggling to catch up.

"I'm sorry... what? Why would you quit your job right now, Marcus? How are we supposed to survive? We have bills to pay!"

"Somebody was stealing. They tried to pin it on me. I'm over that shit. Fuck it. I got something else coming," he explains, still calm.

I sit in that response for a few seconds. Silent. Burning. "Okay, Marcus. Well, thank God the pastor's wife hired me at the daycare. I guess we will figure it out."

What else am I supposed to say? It is... something.

Barely. I work for minimum wage.

The minimum wage is $5.15. Five dollars. And fifteen damn cents. I work open to close, 8 a.m. to 10 p.m., Monday through Friday. And we're still behind on everything. If all my checks are going to the household, where is the money going?

Is this it? Me holding the whole thing together with the equivalent of lunch money. While he's jobless, waiting for some new "opportunity," like jobs are disposable these days.

I guess I'm living that fairytale I dreamed about.

I turn over, pull the blanket up, and pretend it can protect me from what we just stepped into.

CHAPTER EIGHT – SWEET ADDICTION

I don't know what life means outside of being a mom, a wife, and an employee; three roles that don't feel like me anymore.

Marcus? The man's showing his real ass more every day and tightening the leash.

His new obsessions? I can't wear my hair the way I want. 'Natural only' is what he prefers. Like if I'm not natural, I'm not a "real woman."

He digs through my stuff like a damn detective, tosses my hair products like trash. Throws out my clothes because "they don't fit who I am now," or at least who he thinks I should be. He even tore up my senior book from high school; says he can't stand memories that don't involve him.

One day, I wake up feeling like I need a fresh start. I don't have control of much in my life, except...my hair.

While Marcus is at the gym, I walk into the bathroom and grab the scissors. Terrified, I cut my hair down to about 2 inches long as No Doubt Plays in the background.

I run a hand across my head and laugh to myself. "Tuh, can't braid this."

When Marcus comes home, he tosses his jacket on the chair.

His eyes land on me, and in an instant, his face turns.

"Saliya, what the fuck did you do? I didn't marry a damn man! What the hell is this?"

I tilt my head and grin a little.

"Well, you didn't like the braids and stuff, Marcus. I kinda like it." I rub my hand over my head. "You don't like it?"

His jaw tightens.

"Yo, get the hell outta my face. I can't even fuckin' look at you right now."

I lift my chin and walk proudly toward the bedroom.

Suddenly, glass explodes against the wall by my head and shards sparkling across the floor.

I freeze. Heat burns up my throat.

"Did you just throw a damn glass at me? Marcus! Grow the fuck up! It's hair; it grows back!"

I sprint the rest of the way, slam the bedroom door, and I crawl in bed in disbelief. Between fight and flight, my desire to leave feels heavier than ever.

It's May 28, 2005, a Saturday, and Marcus and I are in bed. I'm staring at the ceiling, building up the courage I need in this moment because deep down I know I'm doing it.

"Marcus?"
He looks over his shoulder real slow, like he already knows I'm about to set something on fire.
"Yeah?"
I can't tell if he's expecting bad news or if I'm just projecting... because I know I'm about to drop a bomb

I swallow hard.

"Marcus, I... I cheated on you while you were in military training. I'll leave if you don't want to be with me. I understand."

The confession is blunt, emotionless, each word heavier than the last, but I hope he says get out.

He looks past me, not at me, jaw locked, face blank in that dangerous way I've learned to pay attention to.
Then he laughs once and drops his head like I just said a joke, and it had finally landed.

"Wow. You finally said it, huh?"
He looks up. The smile is gone.
"Yeah... I heard you were being a fucking hoe while I was gone."

I blink, slowly, trying to make sure I heard him right.

"Um... who told you that?"

"Don't worry about it. Just know I knew the moment it happened. You're so damn dumb. I married a dumb ass hoe."
He leans closer. The bed creaks, and he whispers.
"But it's all good, Saliya, you ain't going nowhere. Try me. You wouldn't even survive without me."

I lean in to match his energy. "First of all, Marcus, I'm not dumb. Second, not to be funny, but *you* wouldn't survive without *my* paycheck, because you know —"

63

I don't even finish the sentence before his hand flies toward my face.

I jerk back just in time, and the backhand misses me by inches. I still feel the air shift, the heat of his hand grazing my cheek like a threat sinking into my heart and mind. My breathing pauses, and we both freeze.

He's stunned that I moved, but I'm stunned that he even tried to hit me.

The look on his face changes.

First shock, then shame, then softness, that fake-ass softness. I gather the blanket and crawl to the edge of the bed, trying to peel myself out of this bad dream.

"Damn, I didn't mean to…" He apologizes quickly, like it's going to undo what just happened.

But no, I know better.

I know what comes after the first "almost" and the first apology. I can smell the next scene before it even starts.

"Marcus, if you don't wanna be with me anymore, I'll leave. Tonight. Right now! I'll walk out that door and won't look back. But don't you ever, EVER raise your hand to me again," I warn.

He rubs his face, like he's trying to wipe the truth from his skin.

"No. Let's work through it, Saliya. I... I don't want you to leave. Please, sweetie. It won't happen again," he pleads.

I nod. Once. Quiet. Cold. "Okay."

But it's not okay.

And I know now: if his first instinct is to hit me? The apology doesn't mean shit.

CHAPTER NINE – RUN, RUN, FAST AS YOU CAN

The next morning, while Marcus is at the gym, I make a split-second decision.

I pack a small bag, pick up Nicole from her crib, and buy a one-way bus ticket back to Virginia.

Marie agrees to drop us off at a run-down hotel near the bus station. The room smells like mildew, and the curtains barely cover the cracked windows, but it's close enough to walk, and I don't have the energy to care.

Nicole is sleeping peacefully, curled up beside me, getting the sleep I wish I could get right now. I'm wide awake, staring at the ceiling with every thought running through my head, mostly afraid of what's next.

What was Marcus's face like when he realized we were gone?

I don't want to disappoint him.
Did he flip the mattress? Tear through the closet.

I hurt him badly. SHIT he hurt me.
Is he crying? How mad is he going to be when I
don't come back?

I feel a sense of unease, but I shake off my thoughts, and I pull Nicole a little closer.

All night, I watch her tiny chest rise and fall while I think of what's next for us.

She laughs in her sleep, plays with her little fingers, then sighs and drifts deeper into her dreams like her one-year-old life is full of nothing but love and light. And in her world, it is. I'll do anything I can to keep it that way.

We board the bus early the next morning. Twenty-eight hours on a hot, filthy bus. The seat is sticky, the air stale. A mix of urine, sweat, and too many tired lives pressed together. I hold my baby girl close and force myself not to gag. We push through because what other choice do I have?

I don't sleep. I just stare out the window, letting the blurry landscape roll past as I try to convince myself I'm doing the right thing.

Every bump, every brake, shakes
something loose in me.
And I can't help but wonder:

*Is this what it felt like for my grandmother
the day she walked away?*

Did she stand in the doorway of her house
with twelve children behind her, wondering if
she was brave or desperate, or both? Did she
swallow her fear the same way I'm swallowing
mine now, trying to save herself so her eight
daughters and four sons might have a chance at
something better?

Grandma divorced my grandfather before
I was born, or maybe I was too young to
remember. All I know are the whispers I wasn't
supposed to hear.

Stories of her being found bloody and
broken… bruises blooming across her skin like
dark flowers. A bathtub that could've been her
grave if she hadn't fought her way back to the
surface. If she hadn't chosen to stay alive.

And Momma carried her own version of
that hell.
She survived abuse as a child, then married into
more of it. She raised us alone even when she

wasn't technically alone. She tried to love us with the scraps she had left, her heart stitched together in places I didn't understand as a child.

For years, I resented her for staying. Resented the way she settled, resented the way she put "enduring" before "living."

But now… sitting on this funky ass bus, in the middle of my own brokenness…
I understand her in a way I wish I didn't.

I'm angry; angry that this is what I inherited.
Angry that this is the blueprint.
Angry that survival keeps getting passed down like a family recipe.

Am I breaking cycles?
Or am I running scared?
Am I building something new… or dragging another chain behind me?

The questions claw at me until I look down at Nicole sleeping in my lap.
Her tiny hand curled around my shirt.
Her breath warm against my arm.

And just like that, the spiral stops.

She stirs when the bus hits another dip, sighs softly, and snuggles deeper into me. The bus rattles beneath us, carrying us away from a life I wouldn't have survived much longer.

I let out a breath.

Maybe I don't know where we're headed. But I hope we're going somewhere she deserves.

"I am the safest place she knows. Wow," I whisper, covering her feet with her blanket. Maybe this time will be different. Maybe it ends with me, because I'm not waiting around to see what happens next.

When I arrive in Virginia, I take a couple of steps off of the bus and I'm vomiting in the parking lot. The smell, the stress, the nausea, it all hits at once. I stay for one week, but my family encourages me to try again, and so I do.

They don't know what I know, and I can't tell them. Not right now.

I fly right back to Oklahoma, and I find out I am pregnant again. This time with my little Heaven. My heaven on earth. My number 2.

This pregnancy is more difficult than the last. My body aches in ways I don't even have words for. But worse than the physical pain is the constant, crushing weight of everything falling apart around me.

In July, we receive a notice saying that we have to move from our small home, evicted.

I'm in the school-age classroom at the daycare now, trying to appear energetic, but I'm not. I'm smiling through the nausea, attempting to hold it together.

I'm stuck. Stuck with a man who can't stand the sight of me but won't let me go. Instead, he continues to control and abuse me like a puppet on a string. And it's worse now.

"You're a damn whore!"

That's his favorite line, always the first thing out of his mouth when he's mad. It hits like spit in my face every single time; sharp, rotting, empty of truth but full of venom, and I believe it's who I am.

Even on the days when the Oklahoma sun burns through my scalp, and the heat rises above one hundred degrees. I keep going. Walking. We don't have a car.

I walk to the bus stop in the mornings, the city bus lets me off two blocks from the daycare, and then I walk the rest of the way to work. I usually push Nicole in one of those playschool cars as I waddle with my pregnant stomach, sweat rolling down my face.

"Lord, this can't be life," I whisper to myself as I sing Yolanda Adams' Never Give Up.

When the daycare closes at 10pm, I take a taxicab home. It's like clockwork Monday through Friday.

While Marcus sleeps like a baby at home. He's probably in our bed. He's unemployed, and more than likely undisturbed by any of the shit that's bothering my plump ass.

He's home. Home. If you can call it that.

When I walk in the door from work one cool October evening, Marcus sprawls out on the couch, but gets busy once he sees me walk in.

"Mmph, surprise, surprise. He's not in the bed," I mumble under my breath as I change out of my work clothes and into something more comfortable.

I gather the energy to walk into the living room, swollen feet aching, stomach tight with stress. I grab the mail from the coffee table, and my blood pressure spikes.

"MARCUSSSSS!"

I scream, my desperate voice breaking the silence.

"We're being evicted again!!! What the fuck is this? I'm due to have this baby in two months!!! We haven't even been here long!"

The words ricochet through the house, bouncing off the empty promises and my broken dreams. They bounce all the way into the garage where he's working on some dusty used car we bought to prepare for Heaven's birth. I can't even stand looking at him anymore. Home number two gone. Just like that. But not before our sweet Heaven arrives.

I give birth to Heaven December 20, 2005.

Marcus pulls up to the hospital in our new, but more than slightly used car. The car seat is still in the box. It's a little red car. A trash bag, held by silver electrical tape, covered the busted-out back window on the passenger side. I hide the look of embarrassment and sit straight with confidence as they wheel me to the car. I want to cuss his ass out.

The doctors install the car seat with a concerned look in their eyes as I avoid eye contact. Ma'am! I'm worried too! Sitting hunched over from the c-section and waiting to climb inside because it's freezing.

When I get home and check my bank account, I want to cry. I can't believe it gets worse than this. I've been in the hospital for one week, and it's empty. My bank account is empty. I scroll, hoping it's a mistake, but it's not. Marcus took my entire tax refund and left us with $17, gambling it away at the casino while I was in the hospital.

I pick up the phone without hesitation, dialing the first person I believe can get me out fast. "Daddy," I say, fighting to hold it together. I haven't spoken to him in months.

"Can you please buy me a plane ticket back to Virginia? Marcus spent all the money, our whole savings, at the casino. We're about to get kicked out again. I can't... I can't do this anymore."

On the other end, there's no pause, no questions.

"I've got you, daughter. You go back home. Don't let this man keep doing this to you."

And I do just that, after Heaven's six-week checkup at the doctor, I board my plane back to Virginia.

CHAPTER TEN – TURN THE OTHER CHEEK

I step off the airplane in Virginia, February 2006, exhausted, with my babies and this broken body. But I can breathe again for the first time in three years.

Two months later, in April, Marcus shows up, dragging chaos in behind him, and I just can't say no to him.

Before I can even catch my damn breath, before I can figure out how to stand on my own two feet again, I find out I'm pregnant…again. Right before my birthday.

The sound of my momma's voice when I tell her, she's furious, disappointed, and heartbroken. And I don't blame her one bit.

She stares at me across the kitchen, arms folded, Christmas tree lights flickering behind her.

"Again, Saliya? You're pregnant again? In my house? Ya'll have a month to figure out what y'all are going to do," she says, voice shaky.

"I—I don't even know when it happened, Momma."

I know how sex works, but I damn sure wasn't expecting this right now.

I put on a face of optimism through the struggle that isn't changing. Same shit, different year, different day.

It's January 8, 2007, when Marcus starts a management job at Burger King. I move fast, desperate to get something solid under us before my belly gives me away, securing a position as a bank teller later in the same month. For a minute, it feels like maybe we're doing it, like maybe stability is finally ours.

We move into a big, beautiful home in Yorktown, tucked behind tall oak trees with branches that stretch wide, ready to keep our violent secrets. It looks perfect, always does with him. But inside, I never feel comfortable. I don't even want to fully unpack. I don't trust it.

We settle just long enough for another rug to be pulled out from under me. I give birth to Christina in August 2007. It's my third C-section, my body still aching from stitches and sleepless nights, and the eviction notice arrives. The words blur on the page, but the meaning cuts clean: *out, again.*

I'm devastated, and I can't believe I thought this was going to work out.

I have nothing left. Every month is a war zone, even when I hand over all of my checks. The overdraft fees stack like bricks, higher and heavier, until I can't breathe under them. The late notices scream from the mailbox louder than Marcus ever does, and I don't have the strength to argue over a paper or with this man.

We pack up again, stuffing our lives into boxes that smell like stale tape and resignation.

I feel so discouraged.

We're leaving a quiet, manicured neighborhood in Yorktown. A place with sidewalks, freshly cut lawns, and the illusion of stability. Five miles later, we settle into a townhouse in Newport News.

The walls are off-white but feel gray. A smaller home in a humbler neighborhood, yet the same unhealthy marriage. Every room, another stage for his damn rage.

Some days are good, but they don't make up for the bad ones.

Arguments escalate, leading to physical violence, or verbal abuse in the bedroom. His words hit harder than fists, screaming names so vicious they bruise deeper than skin.

When I catch my reflection in the bathroom mirror, I see the red marks rising, but it's the echo of his voice that lingers longest in my spirit. I paint on makeup, pull on fake smiles, and step out like nothing's happening.

Every day I struggle to rebuild what he keeps tearing down, me. And it only gets worse after he quits his job managing Burger King. Yep, he quit, another job.

I drag myself to work every morning, hand over my paycheck every two weeks, while he sleeps until noon and wakes up looking for a fight.

CHAPTER ELEVEN – BREAKING FREE

It's Sunday, June 8, 2008, and I'm in the kitchen cleaning while the kids nap. The late afternoon sun filters through the blinds, streaks of reddish-purple light cutting across the walls. The faucet drips in the silence, every drop echoing louder than my breathing. My arms ache as I dump the dirty mop water down the sink, but I don't stop.

Marcus's cologne hits me before his voice does; simmering, and ready to boil over.

"Are you stupid, Saliya? Why the hell are you dumping mop water in the kitchen sink? You're going to ruin the pipes!"

I sigh, already exhausted from cleaning.

"Look, Marcus, I wasn't thinking. I just want to clean up. Please don't start with this right now."

"That's your damn problem."

He slams his fist on the counter so hard the dish rack rattles. The sound makes me jump, but I avoid eye contact.

"You never think! Always doing dumb shit and making excuses for it."

I turn to face him, trying to keep my voice steady and low because I feel in my gut what's coming.

"Marcus, it's not that serious. Let's drop it, okay?"

But he doesn't stop.

"Were you thinking when you ran off with that dude while I was away in 2003? Huh? You weren't thinking then either, were you? Slut! Who's going to want you? I don't even want you!"

My ears burn as the emotion builds.

"Marcus... how many times do you want me to apologize for something I did when I was eighteen? You married me one week after I turned eighteen! It was a mistake, and I'm sorry. I've been sorry for years!"

He steps closer.

"You think I can forget it? Because you're sorry! Yea, you are SORRY! A sorry-ass hoe. You think I'll ever get over the fact that another man touched you?"

I try to walk around him, toward the stairs, but he grabs my feet, yanking me to the ground.

My face hits the steps with a sickening thud, and I roll over.

Before I can recover, he slams my head against the steps again.

I stay silent. Fighting back isn't an option. Not anymore, I'm too tired.

He sneers down at me.

"You're lucky I'm patient enough to put up with your shit, Saliya. You should be grateful I haven't left your sorry ass."

Then he walks away.

When he's done, I pick myself up. My body is too full of adrenaline to feel any pain I take a hot shower, scrubbing until my skin stings, until the steam feels like it could melt the whole moment off of me. It doesn't.

Then I crawl into bed next to my abuser.

The same bed where, on a good day, we make love.
And on a bad day… he makes me suffer.

I go to sleep that night thinking of an escape plan, though I'm not sure of myself.

The sleep isn't sleep at all. It's a restless battle of running. Tornados are chasing me, feet pounding through endless streets, fear clinging until my alarm screams before the sun can even stretch itself awake. I groan, body aching from exhaustion, begging the clock for just a few more minutes.

I roll over, and there he is, Marcus, knocked out cold, mouth wide open, snoring like a damn train.

"Must be nice," I whisper as I rub my eyes and shake his shoulder.

"Marcus... Marcus! Can you help me get the girls ready this morning? I'm running late."

He doesn't open his eyes.

"Nah. I'm tired," he mumbles, turning over and pulling the blanket over his head.

I stare at him in disbelief.

"Typical."

I should punch him right on his damn chin.

No job, yet refuses to help with the kids, even on a morning like this. He can at least keep them home to save us some money, but no. They have to go to the sitters.

One by one, I bathe and dress Nicole, Heaven, and little Christina.

Nicole is four years old, curious, and chatty. Heaven is two years old and has a fire in her even at this age, sharp, bold, and expressive. Then there's Christina, my tiny baby girl. She is 10 months old and loud, though she looks smaller. Her digestive issues keep her from growing like she should, but her spirit is strong.

Between onesies, ponytails, and breakfast crumbs, my mind is racing. I'm thinking about yesterday's fight, unpaid bills, grocery shopping, and how tired I am. I didn't even sleep enough, and I can't remember if I turned off the bedroom light before shuffling everyone downstairs.

"He's right there in bed," I mutter, tightening Christina's diaper with more force than necessary.

"He doesn't even lift a damn finger."

But then I pause, sigh, and look around at my girls. I exhale with a slight smile as I snap myself out of my thoughts.

"What's next, God? Show me something, please lord. I'm tired."

Already running behind, I gather their little jackets, scoop up the diaper bag, and shuffle them out the door like a small parade of resilience and sweetness. I walk them up Aunt Cynthia's porch on Madison Avenue, in a quiet corner of Southeast Newport News, and I rush off to work.

CHAPTER TWELVE – FIGHT BACK

My thoughts don't slow down on the way to work. Even without music playing, there is no silence, just noise.

The sky is gray, with a fog hanging low in the air. It's not too warm. It's an unusually cool June day. Not quite summer. I climb the steps to the bank and drag myself inside as my body goes through the motions.

Sit.

Smile.

Count.

Smile.

Count.

Then I hear it.

"Saliya, you got a call!" My supervisor calls from the back office.

I suck my teeth.

"Already? Who the hell…"

I push up from the chair, "Girl, it's too damn early for somebody to be asking for me." I grab the phone.

"This is Saliya," I say, dry as hell.

Then, the voice on the other end of the phone snatches me out of my workday haze.

"Saliya! It's Aunt Cynthia. Where's Christina? Did you drop her off this morning?"

My breath catches in my throat, and my heart drops. My body turns to straight ice. I don't answer. I can't. Because the second she asks, I already know.

Before my brain can catch up, the phone slips from my hand like it's on fire, smacks the wall, hits the floor, and I'm gone.

I bolt out the office door, through the bank, and down the stairs. My legs don't run; they fly. I swear I don't even touch the ground.

I yank open the car door, and there she is, Christina. My baby. My sweet girl. Knocked out in her car seat, sleeping.

A sob rips out of me so loud I don't recognize it at first. I grab her, pull her into me like I just gave birth to her right here in the parking lot.

She stirs a little, then looks up at me, all groggy and soft, like everything's okay. Then I see her smile, that little gummy smile I love so much. She doesn't even know I almost lost her. But I'm not okay. It's not okay. It's not.

I hold her tighter and tighter. My tears fall on her blanket, soaking into the cotton like prayers I'm too ashamed to say out loud.

"I'm so sorry, Christina." I whisper, voice torn to shreds.

"Momma will never, ever let that happen again. Never."

I can't even process one emotion before the next one hits: fear, guilt, relief, shame, rage, gratitude, love...all of it. All at once.

This could've ended so differently. What if it had been too hot or too cold that day? Or if Aunt Cynthia hadn't called? What if...

I take Christina up to the bank so that I can close out my drawer and leave for the day. After picking the girls up from Aunt Cynthia's, I drive in heavy silence. I continue to glance at them in the rearview mirror. Nicole is humming. Heaven is staring sleepily out the window. Christina is sucking her thumb while her other hand twirls her shoelace, which reminds me to break that habit.

As I pull into the complex, the sun slips behind the buildings. The air is breezy and so I tell the girls to grab their jackets. I park and step out of the car, trying to gather myself as I unbuckle Christina's car seat. I haven't heard from Marcus all day, and I haven't even attempted to reach out. My phone died hours ago, and I don't care because I need the silence.

I don't have a moment to settle when I hear tires screeching around the corner. The noise is so sudden it feels like it splits the air in two.

My stomach drops, and I turn.

There he is.

Marcus's car is barreling toward me.

I scramble to close the car door. I don't have enough time to get in. "No. Not now. Not in front of them," I whisper, panicked.

He slams the car into park and jumps out of the car, his face already twisted and dark.

"Why the hell you ain't call me all day?"

"My phone died, Marcus," I say, keeping my voice low as I back toward the car door. My hand is flailing behind me trying to find the door handle, and I find it!

"Marcus, you didn't even ask if I was okay! You don't even know what happened today!" I shout as I scoot back into the car, desperate.

"Bitch don't play with me," he snaps, grabbing my arm so hard I can feel my pulse thumping beneath his fingers. I can feel his breath hot on my face.

"Saliya! You got these people out here thinking I'm the enemy? You think you better than me now?"

"Let go of me!" I grit my teeth, tugging at my arm. "You're scaring the girls!"

But he doesn't.

He yanks the door open and hauls me out like I weigh nothing. My knees hit the gravel first, skin scraping open.

"Marcus, wait! No!"

I scream as pain shoots up my legs. I collapse onto my back, hard. Tiny stones dig into my scalp. My head bounces off the concrete with a sickening thud. For a split second, everything goes white.

When my vision returns, I hear my babies screaming.

"Mommy!" Nicole shrieks, her voice thin and breaking. "Mommy, stop Dada! Stop!"

I turn to see Heaven pressing her face against the window, hands pounding the glass, sobbing silently. Christina's wail cuts through the chaos like a siren.

Cars pass. Windows up. Not a single person stops.

"Please!" I scream, my voice cracking, trying to lift my arms to shield my head. "Somebody help me!"

Marcus's fist connects with my cheek. Once. My teeth clack together. Blood fills my mouth, mingling with the scent of hot rubber from the nearby tires.

I don't think. I just move.

I push off the gravel, palms slick with dirt and sweat, legs like lead. I scoop up the kids as Marcus lunges again, hands tearing at my clothes.

"Don't touch them!" I scream, voice ragged.

Christina's tiny hands clutch my shirt as I hold her to my chest. I shove Nicole and Heaven toward the road.

"Run!"

He's right behind me. Each step cracks against the pavement like gunshots. Even in his rage, he's careful with Christina in my arms.

Out of the corner of my eye, I spot Mr. Ellis, our neighbor; the one I wave to every morning on his way to work, he slows his car as he catches the chaos unfolding.

I wave him down, desperate. He pulls up just enough for me to yank the door open.

I scream as I push the girls inside the passenger door. They jump into the back seat as I try to close the door behind us.

"Drive! Please, drive now!"

Marcus sees an opening and grabs my legs, fingers digging into my ankles. His grip is so tight my foot goes numb. I brace my back against the seat, wedging both feet against the doorframe as he tugs harder, dragging me inch by inch toward him.

Then his shirt flies open, and I see it; a gun tucked in his waistband.

Time halts. My breathing is deafening.

I don't know if I'm gasping or screaming, but the driver must see it too, because the car launches forward so fast my head snaps back.

The tires screech. The door slams shut on Marcus's hand, ripping his grip away from my pant leg.

We speed off.

I'm crumpled in the seat, clutching my belly, chest burning. No one speaks.

The girls are crying, tiny voices cracked and scared. I reach back while still looking forward, fingers brushing their legs to feel them there.

We don't stop until we pull into the police station, and I'm shaking so badly I struggle to get the door open. An officer helps me out while the driver, God bless him, rushes to explain everything.

They sit me in a small, cold room with white walls and soft voices. A woman looks me up and down and slides a pamphlet across the table.

"Saliya, what you've experienced… this is abuse. Physical, yes. But emotional, too. Psychological. You don't have to carry this alone. Please take these pamphlets and consider joining a group for victims…"

I nod, trying to follow her instructions, protocol, but my ears ring and my mind feels foggy. I grab the information and leave.

I don't want to talk or relive it. I don't want pity, analysis, or labels. But the state takes over, pressing charges, issuing a two-year protective order, and restricting Marcus from carrying a gun.

At least, that's what they say.

Marcus has to spend the weekend in jail, giving me time to plan my next move. When I return home, I send the girls inside and dial someone I trust: my old pastor.

"Apostle… I don't know what to do," I whisper, "Am I being punished right now? After what I did… do I deserve this?"

"Saliya, no one deserves to be hurt. Infidelity is wrong, yes, but so is abuse. That is never the answer. Marriage is about love, forgiveness, and growth, not violence and control." His voice is steady and kind, but I struggle to accept the words as I tighten my lips.

"But I hurt him so badly, Apostle, and I don't know if he'll ever see that I always wanted to fix it."

"Saliya, right now, you're going to have to leave for your own safety. You can't keep living like this."

Safety. The word slices through the fog in my head. I repeat it, over and over, letting it root itself deep inside me. I hang up and inhale, trying to catch my breath. Some of the weight lifts, just a little, but it's enough.

I run inside, grab the keys to the red two-seater truck Momma let us borrow. After I pack the girls, toss three car seats in the back, pile in a few trash bags of clothes, I run.

CHAPTER THIRTEEN – DAMAGE CONTROL

On the way to Momma's house, I call Marie. She always knows what to say, and right now, whatever it is, I need it. She can cuss me out; I just want to hear her voice.

"Marie, Do you know we got evicted from every house we lived in? Every car we had, repossessed. Girl, who the fuck am I? I caused all of this, honestly. My momma would've beaten his ass down a long time ago for putting his hands on me, had she known."

Marie and I laugh for a moment before she lays into me.

"Listen to me, Saliya. That voice in your head? The one telling you this is your fault? It's lying. You made mistakes, sure, but don't confuse guilt with responsibility. He chose how he treated you. Fuck that man. You didn't cause this. And listen, you don't need to have it all figured out right now. Just keep driving and get to your momma's house so y'all can be safe."

I wrap my hands around the steering wheel a little tighter. Marie's right: I don't have all the answers. And that's okay.

The girls bounce around in the back seat, squealing now because they know we're going to Nana's. I hope they forget about this night.

I don't want them to grow up remembering that time when their father was mean to their momma.

It's over. It has to be.

After putting the girls to bed at Momma's, I sit in her living room. The space feels worn, but comforting, like the old T-shirt my auntie gave me when I was in elementary school. It was too big then, but now it fits just right.

That's how Momma's house feels now, It was too big then, but now, it's just right.

The soft humming of the ceiling fan that fills the quiet night is comforting, and I can hear the occasional whimper from Christina in the second bedroom. Before I even moved back home, Momma set up that room for the girls. It's her way of always being prepared, always thinking ahead.

The girls are finally asleep after their long day; tiny voices replaced by a peaceful silence.

I curl up on the couch with a cup of coffee, smelling the apple cinnamon candles that wrap around me like a hug.

Momma is across the room, in her usual spot. She's half-watching F.R.I.E.N.D.S., a show we've seen countless times. We still laugh at every joke. Her presence is steady, a silent reassurance that no matter how messy my life gets, she's here.

Momma's one of those women whose strength speaks louder than her words. Or maybe her words match her strength?

I'm thankful that while I was away, she put down the alcohol and left my step-dad, and I couldn't be happier. It was a battle I probably didn't need to be around to witness. And she's better for it.

At 5'7", her slim frame seems almost regal but intimidating. Her brown skin glows even in the soft light of the living room. Her tapered haircut is sharp and unapologetic, like her personality.

She has a way of carrying herself that lets you know she doesn't play about herself or her family. She will knock you out, and I've always loved that about her.

My friends always feared her growing up, and I couldn't blame them. She has this no-nonsense demeanor, but when she smiles with those dimples, when she lets it out, it melts the hardest hearts. Beautiful.

"I wish it didn't have to be like this, Saliya, but I told you that man wasn't good for you."

She's stern but soft, carrying the weight of everything she's been through, knowing that I'm going through the exact same thing.

I swirl my coffee, knowing that she saw something I didn't see when I was 14 years old. I trace slow circles in the cup, eyes fixed anywhere but on hers, letting shame seep into every corner of me.

"Momma, I don't even know why I stayed so long. I really wanted the kids to grow up with a mom and dad in the same house, you know? I feel so stupid for thinking it would get better."

"Saliya, don't you ever call yourself stupid."

Her eyes narrow in on me.

"You're not the first woman who stayed too long, and you won't be the last. You loved a man, that's all, and you did exactly what you saw me do."

She takes a slow breath, her gaze drifting off, distant, as if she's somewhere else for a moment. Then she turns away from me.

"You stayed too long in a space you knew you didn't belong. Like I did with David."

Her voice drops on his name, the regret curling around her words like smoke.

My stepdad, David, was about 5'6". Dark skin. His stocky build made him seem larger than life even though he wasn't that tall. He kept a high-top fade when I was younger but cut it lower to keep up with the times, I guess. But it was his laugh, that loud, cackling laugh that you'd hear across a room and know it was him.

Despite what he felt was "charm," David was complicated. His presence in our family was steady but distant, more so tolerated than embraced.

I'd never felt close to him, and I don't think my brother did either. He was there because Momma loved him, and for a while, it was enough for us. But their relationship was volatile, the love that leaves scars, mental and physical scars.

I'd seen it as a kid, and it left a mark on me I was only beginning to understand now, as an adult.

I lean back on the couch, my coffee cup warming my hands, but I still avoid Momma's eyes.

"You know what I'm going through, Momma," I say, taking a careful sip. "You've been there too."

"Yeah, Saliya, I've been there," she replies, "and I came out on the other side! You will too!"

Her words comfort me a little, but it doesn't touch the guilt I feel. Still, I hold on to them, hoping she's right.

I saw the exhaustion in my momma's eyes growing up every day, and it made me feel two things at once: grateful and sad. Grateful for everything she did for us, and sad that she had to bear so much. It was a constant tug-of-war between love and pain, and it shaped how I saw her, how I saw myself, and...how I saw love.

I not only witnessed the domestic violence, but I inhaled it, multiplied it, and carried it into adulthood, tucked into my expectations of what love looks like, what I would accept. But now I see the pattern. I see how generational pain and abuse bleed down until someone breaks the cycle.

A few hours pass, and the weight of the day still lingers, but it's no longer unbearable. After a quick conversation with Marie, I hang up the phone and fall asleep quickly, thankfully.

CHAPTER FOURTEEN – AFTERSHOCK

I'm feeling a little brain fog, but I'm excited to be at the farmer's market with Marie. As we walk, I close my eyes and take in the scent of ripe peaches and fresh bread. The noise from both the vendors and customers echoes like surround sound. Marie's laughter mixes with the sounds of everyday life, and it feels normal, light, and safe.

But then the wind shifts quickly.

A low howl moves through the market, pulling at tablecloths and sending loose napkins spiraling into the air.

"Hey! Watch out!"

The vendor shouts as a basket of apples tumbles to the ground. They roll over the pavement like marbles, scattering in opposite directions.

"My table!! Catch my table!"

Marie grabs my hand.

"Sis, let's get inside. I think a storm is coming!"

Her voice is unsettled and edged with fear as she tries to speak above the wind that's growing.

I shake my head in agreement, but the sky darkens too fast, like an ink spill swallowing the sun.

The wind is roaring like a living thing, tearing through the market. Tents flip, crates smash, glass shatters. I lose my grip on Marie's hand.

"Marie! Wait!"

But when I turn around, she's gone, and I see Marcus rushing toward me with that look in his eyes.

Panic grips me as I spin, searching for some place to hide, and then I see my momma's house in the distance, standing against the storm like an anchor.

The cellar door. If I can just get there.

I try to run, but my legs are sluggish, like I'm moving through deep water. Dirt and debris tear at my skin.

The wind is gradually getting louder, rattling everything; signs, fences, the bones inside me.

The cellar door is within arm's reach; I know I can make it. I throw myself forward, my fingers brushing against the handle as I feel two hands grab me from behind.

I feel the hands dig into my waste and I grimace, and then I'm lifted.

The ground disappears beneath me as the storm wraps around my body, yanking me into its chaos.

I scream, but the wind steals the sound. Spinning, weightless, helpless, gone.

I hit the ground hard, except I don't.

I jerk awake, letting out a shrill scream.

My heart's pumping, my breath coming fast like I've been running.

I blink, trying to shake the weightless, wind-ripping feeling. My room is dark. No flying fruit, no rattling cellar door. Just me, breathing too damn loud in the quiet. I rub my face and exhale slowly.

"Man... these dreams are kicking my ass."
I sit up straight as I exhale, relief. My whole body
feels wrung out, like I got tossed around in that
storm. My legs are still heavy, and my head even
heavier.

It's July, and I've been back at Momma's
for one month, finally settled, finally getting used
to the routine. The heartbreak is fading now
because life has to go the fuck on.

I don't have time to wallow.

To break up the monotony, I decide to
take the girls to the beach, Buckroe Beach, to let
them run and scream, and burn off some energy.
We're stretched out on our towels, the sun
baking the week off of us. It's a last-minute trip; I
didn't tell anyone where we were going.

I lay back on my sand-made pillow,
Listening to Aerosmith's Dream On, half-
watching the girls splash in the shallows, when
my phone buzzes. The screen lights up.

Marcus: How's the beach?

My stomach drops, and I sit up, squinting
against the glare.

"Huh?"

I nervously look around us trying to find him.

Me: What are you talking about?

Marcus: The beach. You having fun?

Me: How do you even know I'm here?

Silence. Just the sound of waves crashing and kids laughing in the background.

Finally, he texts me back.

Marcus: I just know

I stare at the phone like it's going to give me answers. Feeling that fear I felt months ago. The ocean doesn't feel like freedom anymore. It feels like he's everywhere, watching. I hate him for making me feel this way.

I put him out of my mind after that day. He has a restraining order, funky ass piece of paper, but it says he can't touch me. The last time I interacted with Marcus for the sake of the kids, he said he wanted to get the girls for the weekend. He ended up cutting his visit short because he couldn't do their hair.

The girls ask about him less and less now. Nicole still sometimes clutches her favorite blanket he gave her and asks me if Daddy will come to see her "birthday." I can hear in her voice she's understanding we're no longer together. Heaven doesn't say much; she watches me with those wide, beautiful eyes, like she's waiting for my cue on how to feel. Christina is too little to even know what's missing.

I come home to a dark room at my momma's house because she works evenings. I heat leftovers, fold tiny T-shirts in neat stacks, and stare at the TV without watching it. Most nights, I fall asleep on the couch with the light still on.

I wonder if they'll grow up thinking love always looks like leaving, or if they will even know what's missing.

Here's to the new norm.

CHAPTER FIFTEEN – BANK MAN BLUES

It's August, and I'm sitting quietly at my teller desk. The air inside the bank is so cold and clammy against my skin and I'm pissed because I don't even have my blanket.

"Why the hell is it so cold? This isn't the damn doctor's office."

I pull my half sleeves down as far as they'll stretch. It's a sharp contrast to the sweltering heat outside. The faint buzzing of the fluorescent lights and the occasional shuffle of paper are the only sounds keeping me company and awake as I freeze to death.

Twirling my pen between my fingers, my mind drifts to thoughts of moving into my first apartment in October. In just two months, my girls and I will finally be on our own. Pride mixes with boredom as I idly click the buttons on my calculator, making fake budgets based on what I think the bills will look like.

I crumple my eleventh piece of paper when the bell above the door jingles, pulling me out of my thoughts. A deep baritone voice cuts through the quiet.

"Good morning," he says.

Well, damn, Mr. Bank Man.

His smile catches me first; wide, warm, framed by deep dimples.
Then the rest of him follows. He's tall and lean, at least 6'8", light-skinned, dressed in crisp blue scrubs that fall perfectly over a body that's both slim and unmistakably strong.

Mmm, I know he can pick me up.

I try to reel myself back into reality, but it isn't working.

Then his eyes meet mine. My ears immediately get warm.

"I can help the next person in line."

I wave my hand in the air, but then I notice he's the only one standing there.

Embarrassed, I straighten up in my chair, tuck a loose braid behind my ear, and I wave him over. My whole body suddenly feels hyper-aware as he approaches the counter, and my mouth goes dry as hell.

I take a sip of water as he hands over his deposit slip. Our fingers brush ever so slightly. It's nothing, but it feels like everything, and my brain instantly starts singing Phil Collins: *In the Air Tonight*.

Bitch, stop it.

His cologne hangs in the air and pulls me from my thoughts for a moment, a spicy, clean scent that makes my head swim as I continue his transaction. Our eyes keep meeting, holding a moment longer than necessary.

Each interaction within these few minutes feels like an electric jolt, and I can't help but smile every time he speaks.

When he finishes his transaction and turns to leave, he flashes me another smile that sends shivers down my spine.

I grab my face and start singing a little bank man song, laughing at my excitement.

"My goodness, bank man, you look deliciousssss." I haven't felt these feelings in years.

"I think I drooled a little," I admit to myself as I grab a napkin and toss back the rest of my water.

This becomes our routine.

I eagerly expect his visits, watching the door twice a week, Tuesdays and Fridays, waiting for those long legs to appear first. Flirting and a little small talk become our unspoken game. He always comes to my window, sometimes waiting back for me if he has to.

Two months later, in October, he makes his move. He slides a receipt across the counter and leans in, lowering his voice.

"Text me. I want to see you after work today. Meet me on the hospital steps."

My eyes widen as I stare at the ink on the paper. Oh shit. I'm so nervous I feel like I have to pee. It's his number! I tuck the receipt into my pocket and try to maintain my composure as he walks out the door.

The clock strikes 4:00pm, and I lock up, grab my bag, and head to my car. The hospital where he works is only a block away, and it's way more intimidating now.

I pull up and call him; he answers on the first ring.

"Come up the front stairs and meet me by the elevators."

I love the way he instructs me; *mmm!! Say it again*!

Before I can respond, the line goes dead.

"I think I'm going to throw up on this man's shoes, the fuck he got me doing."

When I step through the doors, he's there, standing near the elevators. My smile spreads involuntarily. He leans in. His lips brush close to my ear.

"You gotta act like you don't know who I am."

I raise an eyebrow, amused by his mysterious behavior, but I follow his lead.

The elevator ride is a mix of tension, anticipation, and confusion because where the hell are we going, I still have no clue.

Two other doctors enter the elevator briefly, but they exit on the next floor: it's just us. The doors close, and he gives me a slight smile. His eyes meet mine.

"You look great, just follow me."

He leads me through the sterile hallways of the surgical floor; the smell of the disinfectant turns my stomach a little.

This is not what I had in mind.

Finally, we reach a set of double doors, and he pushes through into an empty room, dimly lit and quiet.

He turns me around gently, placing me on the cold metal frame of the hospital bed.

I grin.

"Oh, we about to play Operation?"

He flashes the cutest damn smile.

"Something like that."

Whew. His voice is so deep it should come with a warning label. His thumb brushes my cheek.

"How'd you get this scar?"

My face goes blank.

"Stitches when I was a kid. Hit the toilet, blood everywhere."

He winces.

"Looks like it hurt if it's still that visible. I'm sorry, baby. Let me kiss it."

"You sure can."

He doesn't say another word.

His warm hands clash with the cold metal of the table, and the contrast sends a shiver racing up my spine. Somehow his touch makes me forget the smell of disinfectant, the hard bed beneath me, everything.

He gathers a handful of my braids, guiding me by my hair, gently back onto the bed. His movements are slow, deliberate, like he wants me to remember every second of what's happening.

He slides his hands down to the waistband of my slacks, easing the fabric from beneath me without removing them fully.

"Unbutton your blouse."

When he says it, my body temperature increases as I reach to my top, not breaking eye contact. I unbutton slowly, one clasp at a time.

His eyes linger on me, watching me move, with a focus that feels like heat.
Then he comes closer, lips to my neck, soft at

first, then deeper, sending sparks straight through me as I feel his teeth and lips like a suction on my neck.

I can't believe any of this is happening, not here, not now, not in the middle of a sterile hospital room I was supposed to feel nothing in. But his touch... his presence... it pulls the world out of focus until all I feel is him and the way he makes everything inside me light up.

Every breath, every brush of his mouth, feels like electricity humming beneath my skin.

When it's over and we're breathing all heavy, I look down in disbelief, speechless. My braids are wild, my body's limp, and I have a dumb radiant glow all over me.

He walks me back toward the elevators like nothing happened, kisses my forehead real soft, points to the exit, and walks in the opposite direction.

Gone...

Gone just like my damn self-respect because what the fuck was that.

GONE.

Saliya, what the hell just happened?

I scold myself with a huge smile on my face, still giddy as I make my way back to my car. The divorce, the heartbreak, none of it matters in this moment because I feel alive. Satisfied and alive, but it doesn't stop there.

By day, he leaves me little notes at my teller window, playful and teasing. At night, we walk along the beach together, the sound of crashing waves and the cool ocean breeze wrapping around us.

We pass those big ass million-dollar homes, and I daydream of what it would be like to own one, one day. For now, though, this is enough. He is enough. It's predictable and still enjoyable.

It's the middle of November now, and the air has that fall crisp to it. I pull up to our spot, the same beach we always walk, where the sand gives just enough to make your ankles complain.

We head toward the water, steps sinking a little until we hit that damp stretch near the edge. It's firmer there, and our footprints press into the sand like proof we were here.

The breeze is salty and full of the ocean's energy. I feel like the main character in a movie as Blackstreet, Never Gonna Let You Go plays from my phone.

Mood set. CHECK!

We finally reach the darkest part of the beach. That's when he stops, turns to me, and pushes one of my braids out of my face like he's been waiting to do that all day.

"You know you're beautiful, right?"

His calm voice makes me uncomfortable for a moment, but then I give in. He's smooth like the waves crashing behind us.

I tilt my head up and let out a soft laugh.

"Yeah, yeah... but it doesn't hurt to hear it again, from you."

His laugh is low, deep. Whew. That sound does something to me. Heartbeat? Skipped. Thoughts? Gone.

"Come here."

He pulls me in.

His hands grip my waist like he knows exactly where I'm supposed to be, right there. His lips meet mine, like he remembered how much he missed me. And I melt.

Next thing I know, we're down in the sand, his fingers sliding through my braids. He kisses me like there's no maybe, no what-ifs, no next time. Just now. It's like the universe knew what I needed and sent it right in. Building me up, and everything else fades out. It's just me, him, and the ocean.

The waves crashing behind us become our playlist as we lose ourselves in each other. And in that moment, I swear, I never want to come back to real life.

CHAPTER SIXTEEN – REALITY CHECKS

About a week later, I meet up with Marie at our favorite café. The aroma of freshly brewed coffee mingles with the buttery scent of pastries. The café is bustling around us, voices low and cozy, plates clinking, baristas calling out names.

She moved to Virginia last month, still finding her footing after her own divorce, but the decision for us to let our kids grow up together already felt like the best choice either of us could have made.

They blend into each other's routines almost effortlessly; bike rides after school, sleepovers, laughter echoing through the house like they'd known each other their whole lives. My girls and her boys.

We've been making the best of a great situation, always kicking it, turning what could've felt like two broken families into something whole again.

The weather has blessed us with a perfect day, overcast, cool, low humidity, like the air itself wanted to give us a fresh start.

I stir my latte absently as we settle into our conversation.

"Marie, girl, this man has me in a chokehold."

I leaning in conspiratorially.

"I see him four times a week. Day, night, it doesn't matter. I'm there. I don't know if it's going anywhere, honestly, I don't even want to know. But girl… I haven't felt this spark in years, since, well, you know… It's so good, Marie. So good."

Marie raises an eyebrow, her lips curling into that knowing smile.

"Well, it's good you're feeling something after everything you've been through. You deserve to feel noticed and appreciated… even if it's sexuallyyy."

She drags that word out with deliberate slowness, and we both burst into laughter. We know exactly what this is.

I pull my coffee in and wrinkle my nose.

"Ehhh, I don't know, Marie!"

"This man has that dangerous, too-good-to-be-true energy. Whew! He got your girl twisted in all the good ways. Figuratively, literally!"

As I laugh at myself, Marie's smile fades slightly, and she leans closer.

"Look, Saliya. I get it. You've been through a lot. When someone really sees you, it's like a light in the dark. But you have to be careful, because these situationships? They can get messy."

Yes, she's right, but I do not want this negativity in my life right now. I want this good loving.

"OKAYYYY, you're right, Marie. I will not ruin my life behind a man, girl, relax." I hesitate, with a cheeky grin, "Even if he has the best penis everrrrr."

Marie's eyes widen, and she throws her napkin at me.

"Okay, first of all, WAY more than I want to know. Second, stop letting good dick cloud your judgment! Vet your men better, Saliya! I'm not your therapist..."

I laugh, sipping my coffee. "But, Marie, it IS—"

"AHT AHT! Shut up. I'm paying for your coffee. Let's go," she says, rolling her eyes as she stands up to pay the bill.

As we walk out, I call after her, "One more time, Marie! And I'll leave him alone!"

Marie glances back, shaking her head.

"Girl, whatever! You know you're going to keep humping on that man!"

The café customers look around at us with disgust at our antics.

Well, she isn't wrong.

That evening, I arrive at my bank man's house. The rain is steadily tapping against my windshield like a calming melody. As I pull into his driveway, I see his familiar car parked and feel my body tighten with anticipation.

He meets me at the car with an umbrella, his broad shoulders filling the doorway as he grabs my bag and ushers me inside. I swear I can see his six-pack through his shirt. *My goodness.*

The warmth of his home envelops me immediately, and I smile when I see a bottle of my favorite red wine on the table, Roscato. Don't judge me. I'm cheap date.

Without a word, we head to the bedroom, the anticipation thick in the air and I already here the music playing, Arctic Monkeys, I Wanna Know.

As he turns me toward him and pushes me to the bed, his shirt is already off, revealing a chest so perfectly sculpted it could be on a magazine cover. My breath increases and my knees weaken.

He traces his fingertips along my skin and then holds my right hand in the air with his left hand, gently releasing it. Touching my fingertips softly with his mouth, he kisses my hand, my forearm, my shoulder. Then nibbles on my neck, back down to my shoulder, and cups my breasts with his mouth.

He twirls over my stomach with his other hand...It is passion unlike anything I have ever experienced. He hovers over me and opens his mouth. My mouth is already open. He lets a slight drip of saliva drip down from his mouth into mine and begins kissing me passionately.

My body shakes as we fall into the most perfect lovemaking session I don't want to let go of, but I know, I know. I have to. Because, like

Marie said, someone is going to end up hurt. And that someone is going to be me.

I want to hold on to this feeling, but it is temporary. Letting go isn't easy, but, eh, my heart isn't broken.

I just needed someone to knock my boots off of my feet. But please, I hope my forever man comes with good dick too. Please...

CHAPTER SEVENTEEN – TWO STEPS FORWARD

It's January 2009, and I turned 24 last month. I have been in this apartment with my babies for three months, cozy and warm. Dinner is prepared and served, and I'm sitting at the dining room table with the girls, quietly admiring their growth.

The soft glow from the Minecraft lamp on the living room table has me in a trance, reminding me that my beautiful girls call this place home.

The light catches the stack of unopened bills, my budgeting spreadsheets, and planner spread across the end table, proof of a life I'm building piece by piece.

I lean back in the chair, eyes drifting to the empty recliner in the corner, and I pick up my phone. I scroll through my contacts, and one name catches my eye: **BankManGoodPenis.**

I pause. My thumb hovers over the message icon. For a second, I imagine what I'd say. What we would do…But then I laugh under my breath and set the phone down.

Growth, Saliya. Growth.

When I glance back at the chair, it's not so heavy anymore; there's hope sitting in it now.

"One day my husband is gonna be sitting riiight there... eating the food I made for this amazing little family."

The weight of the day presses down on me like a boulder; my head is pounding like it might split in two. Still, a small, hopeful grin spreads across my face at that thought. For a moment, everything feels okay. I love days like this. I am tired, but I'm a proud momma.

"Alright, girls! You know what time it is!"

I clap my hands, standing up with exaggerated energy.

"Bedtime for you, me time for your mommaaa! Is everyone showered? Teeth clean? Bonnets on?"

"Yes, Momma!"

They speak in unison, dragging their feet as they shuffle toward their rooms like reluctant little soldiers.

I watch them go with a mix of love, admiration, and exhaustion; their tiny frames disappear down the hallway.

As soon as their doors click shut, I collapse into my bed and sigh deeply. The silence is always a relief, but it also leaves room for my thoughts to creep in.

I'm not even surprised Marcus disappeared. This is textbook him; he's not showing up for the girls, not sending child support, not even pretending to check in. Just radio silence for 6 months straight, out of spite probably.

And honestly? That man barely showed up when we were together, so what was I expecting now? A transformation? From the same man who has been married to his ego since day one?

I catch myself before I spiral, let out a quiet exhale, and glance at the clock glowing on my nightstand.

11:47 PM. Lawd, I'm gonna need an extra-large coffee in the morning. Tuh, I want some Bank Man in the morning.

I smile, thinking about the good old days. Not the relationship ones, just who I used to be when I was carefree and untouchable. But I'm in an even better space now. Clearer. Stronger. Quieter in my spirit. I slide into bed, pull the covers up, and let the silence hold me instead of haunt me.

Morning comes faster than it should. Like it snuck up on me just to be petty.

The usual chaos kicks off; kids yelling about missing shoes, backpacks half-zipped, breakfast I don't even remember cooking. It's a mess.

By the time I've wrangled ponytails and found the last juice box, I'm running on fumes, but I get the kids to Aunt Cynthia and I'm off to work.

I slide my office keys from my pocket and let a small smile tug at my lips. From the teller line to supervisor? Yeah... I built something I can be proud of. Step by step, brick by brick. Every foot closer to that building is a quiet reminder:

You made it, girl. You did it.

But the wind shifts.

Not just a breeze, this is a warning. The kind that rattles bones and glass doors. The sky flips on me, turning dark so fast it steals the sun before I can process what's happening.

I freeze.

A low growl rises in the distance, and I know this sound. It's not thunder. It's a roar. And it's coming. I look up and I see it tearing through everything in its path like it's got a personal vendetta.

The tornado.

Again.

I try to run, but my legs won't move. My body's screaming "go!," but fear's got me locked.

The wind pulls at me like it's got hands, clawing at my clothes, yanking at my hair as my moans and groans ring in my ear.

My keys slip from my grip and vanish into the air like they were never mine to hold.

I fight, I swear I fight. I push forward, one step, then another, the building within reach. My building. Everything I worked for. But the storm gets there first, ripping through it like a lie, shredding everything I built like it never mattered.

Bricks, glass, hope, it all slashes at my skin as I scream, but even my voice gets stolen.

Then I'm in the air. Spinning. Helpless. Like that little girl again. The one who learned how to be strong too early.

My 5:30 AM alarm yanks me back into reality.

I'm sobbing, the sound tangled with the shrill ring, both of us loud, ugly, impossible to ignore.

I jump up, gasping like I just surfaced from drowning. Hands clutching sheets and swiping at my face, heart about to explode. Sweat soaks my blanket, tears already spilling, mixing with breathless panic.

"I can't take this anymore!"

I snap, not just from the dream. From living with this constant reminder that I'm not in control of my mind.

I call the only person who ever helps me make sense of the mess, Apostle.

"I keep having those tornado dreams, Apostle, and it's making me so tired, mentally, I just don't understand. I've had them since I was nine, at least twice a week, and I don't know what they mean, but they scare the hell out of me. There has to be a reason for them because it's the same thing, multiple times a week, all these years."

He exhales slowly.

"Alright, Saliya. Breathe. You're okay. Tell me about when you started having these dreams, what happens in them?"

"Well, I mean, they start out good, actually. I'm always laughing, or with family, or somewhere doing something I love. Then everything flips and I'm running from a tornado, looking for shelter someplace. But the thing is, I never make it to safety. The tornado gets me first, except it doesn't get me because I wake up before it tears me up. Every time."

I pause for a moment. My mind spins backward, rolling through memories from when the tornado dreams first started.

I was 9 years old, in bed on the top bunk. It was my usual spot because if monsters came, they'd get to my brother first. That gave me time to save myself.

Downstairs, Momma and David were starting breakfast. That was her weekend routine. Then a knock at the door, very unusual for a Sunday. I popped up, head close to the ceiling and pony beads clicking at the end of my braids. The moment felt wrong before I even knew why.

Two of my uncles, Clarence and James, stood there with faces that looked broken.

Uncle Clarence took his hat off, turning it in his hands like he was stalling for strength. His eyes finally lifted to Momma.

"Danielle."

The word came out small.

"Someone killed Stephanie last night. She got shot."

Momma screamed from a place so deep it shook the walls.

I flinched, cried, "Aunt Stephanie," as I watched everyone grab what they could before heading to Grandma's house; because that's where we always went, especially when bad news broke. It was where family gathered, where grief and prayer had a room of its own.

By the time we got there, the house was full; aunts and uncles scattered between the living room and Grandma's bedroom. The air was full of perfume, sweat, and sorrow. The older cousins whispered, the younger ones clung to laps and arms.

My cousin Kayla, Aunt Stephanie's daughter, sat on the bed in Grandma's room looking smaller than I'd ever seen her. No tears, just that blank, heavy kind of sadness. I stood in the doorway, wanting to hug her, comfort her, but the words and my feet wouldn't move.

I drifted to the den with more cousins, where *U.N.I.T.Y.* by Queen Latifah played low on somebody's Walkman.

Grandma's cries floated down the hallway, soft at first, then breaking again into sobs that made the whole house ache.

We stayed until the sun went down, until the noise faded, the music stopped, and all that was left inside that house was a quiet sadness.

That night, when I fell asleep, I dreamed I was on Grandma's porch. A black limo pulled up, and the back window rolled down. Aunt Stephanie was inside, glowing in a white gown, her beauty almost unreal. She lay across the back seat like a mermaid, smiling, but her lips didn't move when she spoke.

Her voice came through like a static-filled radio: *I heard y'all looking for me. Tell them I'm alright. I'm okay.*

The window rolled up, and the limo pulled away. I never dreamed about her again.

Two months later, in March 1994, my cousin Andre, Aunt Patty's only son, died in a car accident. My family was shaken all over again.

I was too young to carry a weight that heavy, but I know life changed after that. Momma's drinking went from zero to one thousand overnight.

At first, she drank and cried out for my auntie. Later, she just drank and cried. Sometimes she passed out with the tears still drying on her cheeks.

I tried to make her comfortable, clung to her like a shadow.

Even when she smiled, I could see through it. I was terrified of losing her, while she was terrified of losing herself.

"...and that's when the dreams started."

He let that settle for a moment.

"Well, sweetheart, you're having the dreams because the fear is still in you, it never left.

But Saliya, you're not nine years old anymore. You're not powerless. That fear? It's just old survival showing up again and again whenever you feel overwhelmed.

That's why you keep having the dream. It has everything to do with how you're feeling mentally and emotionally. But sweetheart, now you've got a choice.

You can face it because you're safe now. And whenever you have that dream, just ask yourself what you're overwhelmed with and face it, head on. Use your voice. Stop running. Can't outrun yourself, baby girl. You're safe."

His words strike a nerve, and I exhale slowly, and lighter.

"Wow. That makes so much sense. Thank you, Apostle, I needed that."

Can't outrun myself, hmph.

I let the words sooth my spirit.

CHAPTER EIGHTEEN – FOUR STEPS BACK

My mood can't be broken after that conversation. By the time I arrive at the bank, I have a little pep in my step. By midday, I'm counting my cash drawer for the audit, my hands moving with practiced precision.

My phone vibrates on the counter. I glance at the screen out of habit, and I see a notification. A friend request.

Social Media Notification: Stephen Brooks sent a friend request.

"Oh, shit!"

The words slip before I can stop them, loud enough to draw puzzled stares from the line of patrons waiting for the count to wrap up.

The stack of twenties in my hand slips from my fingers, scattering across the counter like leaves in the wind.

"Sorry, y'all. Stubbed my toe."

My face burns with embarrassment as I scramble to collect the cash.

I tap "accept" on the request with a grin so big it hurts my cheeks. Twelve years. It has been twelve years since I last saw this man.

Do I even have room to be hopeful right now? Ugh....

Stephen and I were inseparable once, best friends during my senior year of high school. I mean until things became awkward.

We were seventeen, standing by his old Honda Civic one Friday night after riding aimlessly around town. It was a quiet evening of conversation, which was unusual for him. Normally, he couldn't stop making me laugh with his constant jokes or chatting about our EMT-B class.

But that night, he was different.

"Everything okay?"

I asked, leaning against the passenger-side door with my purse slung across my body. The warm night air was heavy with the fragrance of freshly cut grass; the streetlights cast a soft glow around us.

He nodded but kept his eyes on his shoes.

"Yeah, I ... umm..."

He cleared his throat and suddenly grabbed my hand. His touch sent a jolt through me, and not a good one. His eyes caught mine.

My stomach twisted because I barely had time to process what was happening. Stephen stood up from the passenger seat and stepped closer, leaning in, his eyes locked with mine.

I froze as his lips brushed mine, and I twisted my head.

"Oh, no. I don't like you like that, Stephen…and you know, Marcusss." I drag his name out before I could even consider his feelings, half-laughing and half-cringing at the awkwardness of the moment.

Well, damn. That's going to hurt.

Stephen stepped back, his face flushing red as he shoved his hands in his pockets. At about 6'4", with light skin, and thick like a football player, it was strange seeing someone so muscular look so vulnerable.

"Sorry, thought y'all had broken up?"

"We did, Stephen, but we recently got back together. I think this time it's for good. I'm excited."

I was trying to convince both him and me.

"You sure about this guy, Saliya?"

His tone turned serious, like he was trying to control his frustration.

"What do you mean by that?"

Since I knew Stephen liked me, suddenly his perspective seemed clouded with jealousy.

"I mean…"

He rubbed the back of his neck, pausing, unsure of what to say.

"I don't get what you see in him. He's manipulative, Saliya. Controlling. I've seen the way he talks to you, like you're … just there for him, strictly for his benefit, he don't get you like I get you. You know that."

My stomach twisted tighter. It was my intuition trying to scream, 'Girl, listen to him! He's telling the truth!' but I shoved it down.

"You don't even know him like that, Stephen."

I turned and walked into my cousin's apartment without saying another word. The kiss, the warning, we never spoke of that night again.

The school year ended a month later, and that was the last time I saw him.

Marcus immediately told me he didn't want me to have guy friends, and I complied.

And now, Stephen, he's back.

I straighten up at my teller window and start investigating to see how he's been holding up after all these years.

His profile picture is a candid shot of him leaning against a car, older, chiseled, and fine.

"Oh my God, Stephen got in shape! Okay, Stephennn."

Then, a message.

Stephen Brooks: It's real. I've been looking for you for years.

Saliya Holden: Yep! It's real. I can't believe you found me! I've been looking for you too, but I'm at work right now. I would love to catch up.

Stephen Brooks: Call me. We can meet later for a second; I would love to see your face too. 757-555-2289

Saliya Holden: Okay, will do! Here's my number, 757-555-1122.

We exchange numbers and agree to meet at the local PBR that evening, and it's freezing, with snow melting from the last storm. When I pull into the parking lot, my stomach flips like I just found out my favorite ex got married on Facebook.

It's just a meeting, Saliya. You are grown. Act like it.

Then I see him.

He's leaning against his car with that same grin from his profile picture, only finer in person. Tall, lean, so fine it makes you forget your damn name for a second. I don't mean to smile, but it just happens.

Before I can say anything, he's already walking over. He scoops me into a big bear hug. My feet are off the ground, and his arms are locked around my waist like he never let me go in his head.

"It's really you," I laugh into his shoulder, "It really feels like we were just sitting in the EMT class yesterday."

"Yes, it's me," he smiles, pulling back to study my face, "and it's really you. I miss this face... and this scar under your eye."

"Yep, still here!" I laugh.

"I need a sponsorship deal from Fenty Concealer at this point."

We just stand there for a moment, laughing, wrapped in whatever this is. We keep it light, a few cautious words, but the energy is loud. Like, if vibes had a heartbeat, it was thumping.

"So, what you doing now, Stephen?" I try to play it cool, but still nosy as hell.

"I'm a firefighter."

I blink.

"A firefighter? Oh, so you out here saving lives for a living? I'm glad to hear you kept going after our EMT class. I realized I couldn't save lives at that level. Would've been a victim too! You trying to be my hero or something?"

I see him blush, soft and serious all at once.

"I missed you, Saliya. Like for real. Let's stop playing; let's plan that date I never got in high school."

"Bet."

I stick out my pinky finger for a pinky swear. Stephen throws his pinky up to match my energy, and we both fall out laughing.

Three months later, it's April 2009, and whew, this man. The connection is smooth. No games. Deep conversations, our own personal inside jokes and trust like I've known him all my life.

He sees me in a way most men don't because he knew me when no man did, in my innocence, and treats me with care just like that. Not like some project or conquest, but like I'm already enough, even on my off days. Still, he pushes me.

"You're capable of so much more, Saliya; don't settle for this shit you got right now. You deserve more."

And the way he says it? I believe him.

By June, I feel like I'm back in control. In control of my life, my goals, my peace. By July, I feel unstoppable.

Stephen helps me pay off every dime of my debt. Then he encourages me, pushes me, to go for another promotion at work. And guess what? I got it; I GET IT, and I no longer need government assistance.

I'm finally building something stable for me and my girls. Stephen comes to the house on his off days, sees our messy morning, and doesn't say a word. He cleans right away. Sometimes when I come home, dinner is already prepared, music is playing, the kids are giggling, and I exhale. And trust me, I reciprocate all the energy because I want him to feel as poured into as he makes me feel.

The kids are with my cousin and her kids for the weekend, and Stephen and I are in my bed, half-watching a movie. For once, the house is quiet.

Then my phone rings. An unsaved number.

I answer.

"YOU FUCKING SLUT!" Marcus's voice explodes through the speaker. "Fucking that man and your kids are somewhere else! Get your damn kids! I see your legs in the air. You are so trifling!"

I jerk upright, heart slamming against my ribs. The sound of his voice, the cursing; it's like a gunshot in the room.

Stephen's head snaps up. "Who the fuck is that?"

My voice trembles. "It's Marcus."

Stephen's jaw tightens.

"Yeah, I knew he was nuts."

He snatches the phone from my hand and unleashes his own fury back at Marcus.

I stumble to the window, pulling the curtain back.

"Oh my God," I whisper. "He's outside. Across the street."

The phone rings again. Over and over. Calls stacked back-to-back, my screen lighting up like a warning siren.

I text: *Stop.*

But he doesn't.

Stephen turns to me. "Saliya, you need to go to the police. Now."

At the station, the officer barely looks up.

"Ma'am, he wasn't on your property. There's nothing we can do."

"So he can shoot me from across the damn street, officer? This is why women die!"

I spin to storm out, tears of rage stinging my eyes.

"Wait!"

The officer calls, running after me, catching my arm before I reach the door.

"Come back, ma'am, we'll take the report."

That day, Marcus officially earns his second restraining order; he's not allowed to call my phone excessively. I had no clue that this even existed, but I'm thankful.

Stephen can lead me anywhere.

CHAPTER NINETEEN – THE FIRST CRACK

It's a warm August evening, and I walk Stephen to the door after a chill movie night because it's humid as hell outside. The kids are still over at Momma's; the house is dim, soft, and still smelling like that bomb chicken Stephen threw down on earlier. I'm full in more ways than one; stomach, heart, body.

"Bye, love. Let me know when you get home, alright? That dinner had me in a chokehold, whew, I'm about to fall straight out."

As I laugh through a sleepy grin, I stretch my arms out for a hug, already feeling that happy flip in my stomach when he pulls me in.

"I will, babe," he says as he leans in to kiss me.

When the door clicks behind him, I admire him as he strolls down the driveway to his car.

I glance around the house.

Okay, now what?

I debate whether I want to crawl into bed or give in to my late-night sweet tooth.

Answer? Both.

I yawn and start toward the kitchen, but halfway down the hallway, I stop dead in my tracks.

"SNACK TIME!"

I yell, like a damn kid, grabbing my keys and wallet.

"A cold soda and some chocolate? Say less, bitch, say less." I laugh at myself as I head out the door, already tasting the sugar rush.

Crossing the street to the gas station, my happy little escape, I'm humming, minding my business. But then my eyes catch something that freezes me mid-step. Stephen's car is at the pump.

At first, I smile, soft and girly. *Aw, there go my baby. Ooh boyyy, look at youuu…* But the smile doesn't last.

My eyes narrow, my gut twists. My feet almost trip over themselves because, hold up.

Why the hell is this man dressed head-to-toe in a full firefighter uniform? Helmet, boots, the whole nine.

Not a jacket thrown over jeans. Not casual and not normal. His uniform looks straight out of the dry cleaner's; pressed and spotless, like he just stepped off a damn calendar shoot. But when he left my bed, he was in a T-shirt and jeans.

My stomach turns, and I know something isn't right.

"Stephen?" I say as I pick up the pace. "Stephen!"

He turns around too fast, eyes wide like I just caught him robbing the place. Then, too quickly, he pastes on a grin.

"Oh hey, babe."

"Umm, why… why do you have different clothes on?"

I scan him from head to toe.

He blinks. Once. Twice. Then forces a laugh.

"Oh, I spilled fruit punch on myself."

I tilt my head.

"Fruit punch, huh? It splashed in your boots too? Hit your ankles?"

His laugh dies in his throat. Tight. Fake.

"Yeah... it was a lot."

The lie hangs between us for a few seconds as I study his face. I can feel my mouth getting dry as my intuition tells me this man is desperately trying to cover his tracks.

"Odd question, but... are you seeing someone else, Stephen?"

He shakes his head too quickly, too hard.

"Someone else? No way. I told you, just fruit punch. This is all I had in the car, and I didn't want to drive home like that."

"Mmm hmm. Yea, okay..."

I nod slowly, but my chest is screaming. My body knows what my heart doesn't want to hear.

And still... I tuck it away. I don't want the truth tonight. Not here. Not under the fluorescent lights of a damn gas station with sticky floors and strangers filling up their tanks. So I bury the questions. I bury them deep.

But burying it feels too familiar. Like the tornado dreams that chase me night after night. I feel that same fear, helplessness, my heart at his disposal. He's the storm this time.

And that's when I remember Momma. I remember the night she finally had enough of David. We had just come back from a two-week family trip when she burst through the door, eyes blazing, and voice shaking but so sure.

"Saliya, I think he's cheating, and I'm gonna find out."

Her determination was a storm that couldn't be stopped. Every evening when he'd claim he was going "fishing," she'd give him an hour, then circle the city like a hunter, starting downtown and working her way out. Until one night, I heard her yell from the living room.

"I found him! I'm about to go there right now! I don't know who the fuck he thinks he is."

My mouth hung open for a split second before my feet were already moving.

"Wait, Momma! I'm coming with you!"

No way was I missing that. Like I said, she's not to be played with.

Sure enough, she was right. We pulled up on a quiet cul-de-sac off 62nd Street, a house tucked behind two enormous maple trees. And there it was, her car, parked out front like a slap in the face. David had his pick of her three cars, and that night he'd chosen this red one, bold as ever.

I looked at Momma. She looked at me. And then she took off.
Her fists beat on doors, windows, and knocked over trashcans around the house until finally the front door cracked open. Just enough for David to slide her truck keys out like a coward and slam it shut again.

The sound of that door closing felt like glass breaking in my chest. Momma turned to me. Her jaw was tight, her voice low, commanding: "Saliya, take these keys and take my car home. I'll be there soon."

"But Momma—"

"SALIYA! GO HOME."

I drove off, heart pounding, leaving her to finish what she had started. To this day, I don't know what went down after I left, but I know it was the end.

I wasn't sad he was gone. Hell, I never cared for the man. But I was sad at how final it felt; how someone who'd been around since my birth could just disappear like we were strangers passing in a grocery store. We had a history, no matter how messy, and just like that... it was over.

So when Stephen swears fruit punch while my whole chest screams liar, I know exactly what I'm doing. I stuff it down. I pack it tight under chocolate bars, soda fizz, and the lies I let myself swallow. Better to rot my teeth than my heart tonight.

CHAPTER TWENTY – THE SECOND CRACK

September creeps in quickly, and I decide I'm going to take the kids to Stephen's fire station for a truck tour before we dip off on a little fall getaway. It's a bonding moment for the girls, and maybe it'll help ease this weird tension that's been lingering between Stephen and me.

As soon as we pull up, he greets us with that sweet smile. The smile gaslights the hell out of my thoughts because I can never even remember why I'm bothered.

"Hey babe! The kids are coming up behind me."

I smile as I tell the kids to run ahead, they're excited to see the big red truck.

I hang back a little, eyes on Stephen, but my head is elsewhere. Something about him feels… off today. Distant. Like he's here, but a part of him is somewhere I don't have access, and I ride for my fucking intuition. She is always on point. Still, I let the moment be.

The kids climb into the truck and their giggles echo through the bay. I watch Stephen as he shows them the bells and whistles of the firetruck, talking that firefighter talk. I'm just admiring my man in his element; charming, calm, knowing exactly what to say.

And for a second, I exhale.

"This is why I love this man,"

I watch from a distance. Letting him have his space. Letting him do his thing.

And then she appears…

"Hi, I'm Charlie."

She steps forward from the back with a smirk plastered across her face. Her eyes flick toward Stephen and linger a little too long for me.

She's slim, pale, and has long wavy brunette hair down her back. Standing about 5'7" and confident as hell, she introduces herself with a tone that feels more like a challenge than a greeting.

Her gaze shifts to me, sizing me up like I'm not even worth her time.

"Bitch, the fuck?" I whisper to myself behind a tight, fake smile.

"Do you like ice cream?" She says.
"Chocolate ice cream is my favorite."

She casually slides another spoonful of ice cream across her lips slowly and into her mouth.

My hand clenches into a fist at my side, one clutching my bag, and I force another smile, squinting just enough to show I peep the shade.

"The kids are really having fun, Stephen. Thank you so much, love,"

I brush past her with a little extra shoulder and give him a kiss.

Her stare follows me, burning a hole in my back, but I wish the bitch would say something else.

The rest of the tour passes in a blur, because now my fight or flight is at ten thousand. The fight is standing tall like, "Say the word, I'll slam the hoe."

Stephen plays the part of the perfect firefighter while I manage my emotions. He lifts the kids into the truck and explains every button and switch.

I continue to replay Charlie's smirk, her deliberate choice of words, and the way Stephen shifts on his feet like he wants to be anywhere but here.

By the time we leave, my suspicions aren't suspicions anymore; they are dark truths, bubbling up like a volcano, and the dots are connecting.

But what's done in the dark always reveals itself in the light.

When I pull up to the fire station two weeks later, who is front and center begging to be a main character? You guessed it, Charlie. Standing exactly where Stephen parks his car, like she's been out here waiting for me to pull up just so I can see her little performance.

The look of determination on my mom's face that night she had a feeling David was cheating flashes in my mind. My face heats instantly, but luckily I have Marie on the phone already talking sense into me.

"Marie, I swear he is fucking this girl, and I'm going to find out!"

"Saliya! You just focus on not going to jail today; the rest is gonna work itself out, girl, relax."

I don't unbuckle my seatbelt. If I get out of this car, I'll cuss her out so bad, the fire department will need help.

I grip the steering wheel like it's her neck as I dial up Stephen, and I dig up the most sarcastic tone I can find.

"Hey sugar foot! I'm here!"

He strolls out all nonchalant, like the parking lot isn't giving Real Housewives of Newport News, Virginia Reunion pre-fight energy.

Charlie trails behind him, looking like a lost, scraggly ass puppy, moving to help him load a couple of cases of water and his bags into the trunk.

Then she does it. She flashes me this smug little smile.

Oh girl...

I roll down the window, smiling just as big and sweet as pie.

"Heyyy whore!"

I give a little wave with two fingers. Nah, this isn't jealousy; something is going on for sure.

Charlie's face tightens. "Excuse me?" She blinks like she's still trying to make sense of what she heard.

"I said, any…more?" I tilt my head, still smiling.

"Any more cases of water?"

"Oh." She clears her throat. "Nope, that's it. Have a good trip!"

And she spins around and heads back toward the building.

I lean back in my seat, cool as hell on the outside. In my mind, I'm picturing myself casually hitting the gas and clipping her in the knee; just enough to humble her, not enough for jail.

But I breathe, relax, and I remind myself that I'm too fine for jail, too grown for drama, and way too intuitive to be losing it over a firehouse groupie. Barely.

The entire ride to the cabin, I see her face; her intentional, devious smile, as The Weeknd's song, The Knowing, plays on the radio.

The trip is so littered with red flags that I can't focus on anything else. I keep trying to fold them up and tuck them away somewhere, so I don't have to look at them, but my damn flag bag is full of his bullshit.

He goes for a jog before I'm even awake. Long solo gym trips throughout the day. And there's an awkward silence that feels heavier than any argument.

On the second morning, I decide to get up early and join him at the gym. But when I walk in, he looks like he's seen a ghost. His jaw tightens, and he won't even look me in the eye; just stares at the TV, pretending to be interested in the news.

"Boy, you don't watch the fucking news," I say, walking over to him.

"You don't want me here?"

I speak louder this time. It's just the two of us, so I'm not concerned with keeping my voice down.

He doesn't answer right away. Just keeps re-wrapping the Velcro on his wrist brace like it's suddenly a damn Rubik's Cube.

"I... I like to work out alone. But you're good."

The treadmill moves under my feet, but I'm not paying attention to it anymore. Every cell in my body is telling me something isn't right.

When we get back to the cabin, I stand in the little kitchenette while he tosses his keys on the counter.

"Stephen," I say, my voice cracking. "Are you… are you cheating on me?"

He looks up, wearing that same blank-ass expression from the gym, like my question is an inconvenience more than anything else.

"Seriously?" He lets out a dry, humorless laugh. "No, Saliya. I'm not."

I blink back tears. "Well, you sure disappeared this morning."

He shakes his head, and brushes past me like I never said a damn thing.

"You're making something out of nothing, and I'm tired. I'm going to take a nap."

I want to scream and flip this entire cabin, but instead I just stand there, speechless. Unsure why this man can't just tell me he's not ready to settle down.

CHAPTER TWENTY-ONE – FOOL ME AGAIN

It's Monday, and the three-day trip ends as fast as it began, leaving me in that dangerous in-between space:

Is he cheating, or am I just spiraling?

Girl, snap the fuck out of it and say something.

I pull into Momma's driveway, and she's already on the porch with the girls, arms wide like I just came back from deployment instead of a weekend getaway. The kids run to the car, laughing and screaming, "Mommy!"

"My Nana's babies! See y'all next time! Saliya, I hope you enjoyed your trip, boo!" Momma calls out, all joyful.

And here come Stephen, loud and wrong: "It was great, Ms. Holden!"

My *face* did the talking for me. I roll my eyes and buckle the girls in like, *Lord, help me keep it cute.*

Because look at this man, this smiling, grinning, lying-ass liar, lying like it's a family tradition.

The next week, I'm standing in Stephen's living room with his dog's leash in one hand and my phone in the other. I casually scroll through social media while getting ready to take his dog out for a walk. It's one of several small tasks I've gotten used to doing for him during his long shifts.

But something's been nagging me all morning; his words from our phone call while I was driving over are still ringing in my ears.

"Don't go in my room; it's a mess. If you need a nap, nap on the couch."

Stephen never tells me to nap on the couch. Ever. And now it's all I can think about. Why even say that, unless you have something to hide?

After I walk the dog, I head straight for his bedroom. I don't even hesitate. It's like I know I'm going to find something, even though I'm begging God not to.

I open the door…Nothing.

Clean room, just like always. This man lives alone and cleans like he's auditioning for HGTV. I mean, obnoxiously clean.

I let out a breath of relief and turn around, ready to give him the benefit of the doubt. But then my eyes land on the closet door.

"Ohhhhhhh hell."
Now it's just me... arguing with me.
"Girl, it's probably nothing."
"But bitch... what if it's *something*?"
I spin around so fast I almost give myself whiplash and make a beeline for the closet.

I slide the door open, and gag.

A black duffle bag. Unzipped. Women's clothes hang out the top of the bag, and I notice a massage table on the side wall.

My hands go on full autopilot because I don't have much time before he calls to "check on me."
I yank clothes out the bag and spread them across his freshly vacuumed carpet like I'm building a damn case file.

I pause for a second to admire his work like a fool. "Aww, the vacuum lines are so perfect."

Then, I snap photos of everything.

For what? For *me.*
Gotta have receipts.

Then I freeze.
"Ugh. A vibrator?!"
Nope. Absolutely not. We are NOT touching that.
That's where I draw the damn line.

When I finish playing CSI: Closet Whore
Edition, I shove everything back the way I found
it, lock up, and get in my car. My heart is sick as
fuck, but my facial expression is relaxed. My
voice? Light.

I call him as soon as I pull off from his
place and hit the interstate, because I've already
got a plan forming. One thing about Momma? She
raised me to think quick on my damn feet.

"Hey, babe! What size shirt does your
mother wear? There's a buy-one-get-one-free
sale at the bargain store, and I wanna grab her
something while I'm getting my mom's stuff."

He falls for it immediately.

"She's a 2X."

Got. Him.
My smile melts right off my face, turning into
smoke.

"So then whose clothes are in your closet, Stephen? Because your momma's back sure as hell can't fit in a small! You're fucking her, aren't you? Charlie? These look like the cheap ass rainbow rack clothes the raggedy heffa wears!"

First, nothing but silence. Then the lies start tap-dancing out of his lying ass throat. Pants burning up!

"Oh, uh… those are… my niece's clothes. Yeah, she's donating them to Goodwill, and I'm just holding the bag for my brother. He's gonna pick it up soon."

"Mmhmm. Now Stephen, why would you be holding your nieces clothes? Her daddy don't have a place to stay? This little trifling, cheap duffle bag couldn't fit in his car? You donating the vibrator too? Or nah!?"

Now every lie is lit up like a neon sign in the dark:
The "extra" toothbrush, the scented lotion he swore was his mom's, the half-used shampoo bottle, it all says another woman lives here.

Why can't I just let go? Is it because I need him financially? I need more…I need more information…

One night I get a random text from Stephen.

Stephen: Hey Saliya, they need me at the fire station for the night.

Me: Hmmm, okayyy. Have a good work shift babe.

After about an hour of restlessness, I dial Marie.

"Marie, I need you to ride with me real quick."

"Girl, where? I just curled up under this blanket and I'm rubbing my feet together. The hell you need?"

"Marie, I'm on a mission."

I hear rustling in the background.

"You're on a mission? Oh, Lord, Saliya. What the fuck, man?"

"Bitch, just ride with me and shut the hell up."

"Ohhh, you really trippin."

We both laugh as I hang up, but the laugh doesn't reach my stomach. By the time she pulls up, I'm already pacing.

"Okay, we need your car."

Marie throws her hands in the air.

"Saliyaaaa! What are we doing?"

"Relax. I just need to ride by Stephen's house. He said he was working, but I think he lied."

"Oh my goodness, I'm going to jail tonight, huh?"

"Marie, NO! Now come on."

When we get closer to Stephen's street, I spot it instantly; his car sitting in the driveway. My stomach drops. "Wow. He's home."

Marie leans forward.

"Wait. What? He is? And you're sure he told you he had to work tonight?"

"Yes! Marie! Okay, turn the corner."

She turns, and that's when I see it: a black car parked in front of his driveway. My chest goes cold.

"Okay, Marie, drive past slowly. I need to pull up the notes on my phone and take down this license plate."

She groans.

"Saliya, I just want to tell you, if no one has told you today, you are fucking nuts."

I smirk, but my eyes sting.

"Yeah, well, I thank my momma for giving me the nutty gift. It's actually a good quality, because clearly this dumbass can't be honest. Now turn around and drive back the other way. Take me home."

We pass again.

My thumb types the numbers on my phone while hot tears slide down my face. By the time I get home, I'm running on fumes. I go straight to the first personal info search website I can find, throw the plate number in, and pay the two-dollar fee.

"Best two dollars I ever spent."

Marie laughs, but when she looks at my face, her smile dies.

"Wow. Amanda Watson. That's who the car belongs to, Marie. Amanda."

The tears spill again. I tell Marie I'll talk to her tomorrow, leave the computer screen glowing with Amanda's details, and I crawl into bed.

That night, the storm finds me again. The sky goes black too fast, the ground stretches long and impossible, and my legs won't move. My voice is gone, swallowed whole by the roar. But this time, it isn't nameless. This time, the storm wears a firefighter's grin and a stranger's perfume. I jolt awake gasping, chest tight, the name "Amanda" tangled in my throat. Another storm, another night. Like Apostle said, I just need to face this mess head on. What am I so afraid of?

CHAPTER TWENTY-TWO – GONE FOREVER

It's Wednesday, March 17, 2010, and I've spent the better part of the last five months trying to convince myself this man is for me. Through all the shame, the lies, and the quiet humiliation of being cheated on, I'm still afraid to be without him, and it's killing me. Most of my growth has been with this man.
That's the part that hurts the most.

Stephen stands from the bed and grabs his jacket.
"All right, Saliya, I'm headed to work for three days this go-round."

I peel a little green sticker from my purse and slap it on his jacket for St. Patrick's Day. "You can thank the kids for that," I laugh. "You need me to bring you anything? Food, drinks, snacks? I'm about to do a little grocery shopping with the girls."

I turn to grab my purse, and a flicker of gold catches my eye in the corner of his headboard.

Wait. Is that... a condom wrapper?

My brain spirals as I try to avoid a hot flash with deep breaths.

"Nah, I'm good tonight, maybe tomorrow."

He walks to the front of the apartment.

I reach down while he isn't looking and grab the wrapper, tossing it in my purse before catching up to him.

"Okay, sounds good, babe. I'm going to go then. You have a good work shift and call me when you get a chance."

I feel sick all over again, but I jump in the car, ditch the grocery run, and I go straight home to the computer. I call Marie.

"Marie! Girl! Bitch! I found a condom wrapper!"

I'm out of breath as my hand reaches for the computer chair behind me, I hear her gasp.

"Whatttttt, Saliya!! Stephen??!"

She's in disbelief, but shit, so am I!

"Yes, Marie! Stephen! What should I do? What should I do?"

My leg is shaking, and I can't stop my voice from quivering.

"Should I say something?"

Puzzled, disgusted, and understandably so, Marie is as clueless as I am…

"Well, I would, but what are you going to say? Girl, at this point just throw hands because this is embarrassing. Want me to call my people to beat his ass?"

I know she's just trying to break the tension, and it works. I let out a much-needed laugh.

"Okay, first of all, no! Girl, just let me figure this out, and I'll call you back."

I hang up the phone and start looking for clues.

I look the empty wrapper over, front, back, front again. But when I turn to the back and look in the corner to the left, I see a lot number.

"Hmmmmm. I wonder if this is good for something…" Oh, it's Saliya FBIya time!

For a moment, I try to talk myself out of going further.

Why am I still doing this detective work? Why do I need this answer to leave him when I already know he ain't shit?

I pause, taking in the moment., then I snap back to reality.

Google: Trojan condoms lot number search

CLICK

Here I am, in sheer desperation, at the Trojan Condom website, sweating. But that little lot number gives me everything I need in a split second.

Manufactured: 09/12/2009

On Store Shelves: 09/27/200

I want to vomit, but I push through. Now, I need to make that phone call.

"Hey babe, do you have a second?" I keep my voice smooth and calm.

"Yea, Saliya, what's up, sweetheart?"

He doesn't suspect a thing. But of course, he doesn't even know I saw the wrapper, let alone stashed it in my purse.

Still calm, I let it all out.

"So, there was a condom wrapper next to your bed, on the floor near your headboard. When did you use that?"

"Oh, that was James' from when I had that party back in March last year…when I first moved to this apartment."

I let him talk, amused at the lie because now I'm supposed to believe his friend was fucking in his bed…

"Well, you know what, I think I'm done with this relationship for good this time, Stephen, because once again you're lying. The condom wasn't even put on store shelves until September, SEPTEMBER! So, why do you feel the need to keep lying to me like this?!? Have the women! Leave me alone!"

"But Saliya! I love—" I hang up before he can say another word.

One month later, April 2010, I've done nothing but oscillated between anger and heartbreak. We have a planned trip to Las Vegas next week; a commitment I made before everything fell apart. Despite my reservations, I still want to go.

We haven't spoken much since the breakup, but not for lack of trying on Stephen's part. Flowers, texts, even showing up at my job once, but I always stood firm on my boundaries when he tested them. TEN TOES DOWN!

Here's to one last adventure.

When the plane touches down in Sin City, my stomach turns from the pit of nerves I feel. The city is loud in so many ways, and lights flicker like promises too bright to last.

Stephen, in rare form, is determined to play the doting partner, overflowing me with attention, spontaneous kindness, and a charm he hasn't used on me in a month. He buys me all new outfits for the trip, gets my hair done, my nails done, and for this moment right here, I choose to forget the pain. I choose to forget the pain because I deserve this moment of untainted happiness.

We stumble drunk over the bridge of The Venetian Resort, gondolas gliding under us like a scene ripped out of a dream I never dared to have. I pause momentarily, caught by the view, and my tears sneak up on me as I take in the moment.

"Wow, this is so beautiful."

I wait for him to respond.
Nothing.

When I look back, I gasp.

Stephen is down on one knee, holding a ring. His face is steady and so sincere.

What the hell? My brain can't catch up, and I feel like I'm watching a movie with no sound.

"Saliya, will you marry me?"

My past flashes before my eyes like a highlight reel built by chaos. The fights, the passion, the confusion, the moments I clung to hope with bloody fingers and smeared mascara. And now this?

Tears come, part joy, part shock, part exhaustion.

"Yes!"

I try to convince myself that this is my fairytale ending. The ring slides on, and suddenly I'm somebody's fiancée in Vegas!

The rest of the trip is a blur of glitter and adrenaline. I have champagne in each hand, karaoke, and Stephen's nonstop declarations of love like he's trying to drown out the past.

And yet, as we stand at the edge of the Grand Canyon, with sunlight kissing our skin and red rocks stretching into forever… my mind is somewhere else, and I hate that for me.

The view is breathtaking, but I can't fucking breathe. It's too much at once. No, wait, I really can't breathe because of the elevation. I think I'm going to throw up.

The doubts in my head and heart grow louder with every loving gesture. And no matter how hard I try to silence them… they refuse to shut up.

I pick up my phone, try to brush off the insecurities, and I record.

"Stephen, do you love me?"

My tone is probing as I turn to him. He smiles with that easy, practiced smile that could charm anyone.

"Of course, I do."

"How much do you love me?"

I press as I hold my phone up to record him, hoping to capture a moment of reassurance I could replay later.

He hesitates and makes a kissy face.

"That's not good enough. That's not…No, babe, it's a video. I'm recording you, and I need you to say words, how much do you love me?"

He places his hands behind his back and starts walking.

"I love you more than life itself, more than all the grains of sand on… on… erf, E.R.F."

He spells it out and I laugh. With tears in my eyes, I continue to record as he talks.

"More than the distance from here to the moon and back. To Pluto and back!"

I raise an eyebrow.

"To Pluto, Stephen?"

He pulls at his jacket collar.

"Yes, to Pluto, that's quite far."

He leans in and kisses me softly on my lips, then grabs my hand with his sweaty palms.

His words are sweet, the kind any woman would want to hear. But beneath the surface, my spirit refuses to let me rest here.

CHAPTER TWENTY-THREE – THINGS IN COMMON

I meet up with Marie at I Do Bridal Boutique on May 23, just one month after getting back to Virginia. The shop smells like fresh roses and new fabric, and the chandeliers sparkle like they've been waiting for someone's fairytale to start.

Marie is already posted up in one of the plush velvet chairs, tapping her acrylics against her phone screen as she sips an iced coffee. She looks ready; locked in and fully prepared to give me all the *ooohs* and *aaahhhs* a girl could ask for.

I step out of the fitting room in the third gown I've tried on; plunging neckline and back out, exaggerated bottom, the dress that makes a statement even if you're unsure what you're saying. I notice Little Big Town's song, Girl Crush, playing as I glance at her nervously.

"Well? Bitch, are you looking?"

I force a smile, and Marie laughs.

"I mean, it's cute. Saliya, it's really nice, but do you even like it?"

I look down at the train spilling across the floor.

"Yeah... I mean, I think so."

"You think so?"

She squints at me and taps her nails on the arm of the chair.

"Girl, that face says otherwise. You look like somebody told you your man just moved to Alaska and he ain't coming back."

Tired and overwhelmed, I laugh and shrug my shoulders.

"I don't know, Marie. I... I want to feel sure."

She leans in, dropping her voice to that patented soul-snatching tone she uses only when she's about to lovingly drag me.

"Saliya, be honest with me. Shit, be honest with yourself. Do you even want to marry him? Because from where I'm sitting, you don't look like a bride. You look like a damn hostage."

She sits back and picks up her coffee.

I smooth down the dress just to keep my hands busy.

"I feel like I should. That's the thing. We've been through so much. All this history… all the time invested…"

I plop down in the chair next to her, and the dress puffs up like a disgruntled bird, hitting me in the face. We both burst out laughing.

"Girl, history don't mean shit if you're miserable. Y'all got baggage. Not a legacy. Figure out what you really want and stand on it; this is your future you're playing with. It isn't a game, Saliya."

I meet her eyes in the mirror.

"I feel like I'm supposed to be happy, Marie." I say, frustrated with myself.

"This is the part where I say yes, you know, and feel grateful, but I just can't get comfortable. I want too though! Girl, I have on a wedding dress! We've looked at venues, already!"

She softens, stands up, and takes my hand.

"Listen to me, you don't owe him your forever just because he showed up with a ring.

Not if you're doing it to prove a point. Not to make up for all the shit he never apologized for."

"I don't want to disappoint everyone. I don't want to start overrrr againnn. My goodness,"

I throw a fake tantrum, patting my bare feet on the ground.

"Fuck everyone," Marie says without missing a beat. "And you ain't starting over. You deserve a love that feels like peace, not penance"

"Ugh."

I frown my face in confusion.

"What the fuck does penance mean?"

Marie grabs my arm as we laugh.

"Girl! You're torturing yourself! That's what it means! And if he cheated before, bitch, he'll do the shit again. Is that what you want?"

I look at myself in the mirror. The dress feels too heavy. Life feels too heavy. He's giving me what I want, but I don't feel the way I should feel, and it's killing me.

"You really think I should walk away, Marie?"

She tucks a stray braid behind my ear as she hugs me from behind, and we look at each other in the mirror.

"You already know what you need to do, Saliya. I'm just here to remind you that you're allowed to do it."

I nod slowly, the truth lands hard and clear.

"Gotcha, sis."

I pay for the dress I love most, and I leave the store, but every time I look at this ring on my finger, I cry.

By June, I fall apart.

Across from me, in the stiff silence of our couple's therapy session, Stephen just... sits there. I wait for his response, watching every twitch of his face.

"Tell me now, today, did you cheat on me?."

He avoids my eyes.

"Saliya, I didn't, I told you that. You know I love you, and I know we can make this work!"

"Nah, love doesn't look like this! Look at me, I'm frantic and anxious all the time because you refuse to be honest with me!"

He reaches for my hand, and I flinch back.

I slide the ring off of my finger and turn to the counselor. I shake my head and wipe away my tears as I place the ring on the table between us.

"Well, I can't do it anymore, ma'am. I wasted your time. Take it back, Stephen, I can't marry someone I don't trust."

Stephen grabs the ring, without another word, and walks out the door.

I'm gutted.

But deeper than the pain is this sick, familiar thought I've never dared touch: *What if this is what Marcus felt when I betrayed him?*

I've never slowed down long enough to imagine how that sat in his chest; heavy, rotting, the way betrayal sits in mine now. It doesn't excuse what he did to me or make the abuse acceptable, but I finally understand what it is to be shattered by someone you trusted.

And I was the one who did that to him. My betrayal of Marcus wasn't just a wound I gave him; it was proof of the wound carved in me long before him.

Karma is a funky-ass hoe, huh?

I scream into my pillow, face soaked, body exhausted.
"This is bullshit!"

More memories of Momma flash through my mind.

My momma did not go through all that mess just for me to repeat the same dumb shit.

As I curl under my blanket for more comfort, I fall asleep thinking about her pain.

I was fourteen, maybe fifteen, sitting on the stairs of our apartment, eaves dropping as Momma cried uncontrollably.

"I found the letters she wrote to him! In his work boot! In the trunk of the car! And they are funky as hell!"

I didn't know who she was talking to, but I had to laugh because his feet do smell awful; she wasn't lying about that. I crept down the steps a little more and froze.

There she was, sitting on the carpet, with an old Christmas popcorn tin in front of her. Cordless phone in one hand, lighter in the other.

Inside the tin, the letters burned, and the flames devoured every lie in them, or maybe it was his truth and Momma's pain.

Her tears streamed freely down her cheeks, glistening in the light of the fire as I watched her curl up on the carpet like a baby. She cried that cry of utter heartbreak, and it pissed me off and broke my heart, because my mother deserved better.

She asked me to sleep in the bed with her that night and asked me to sing the saddest song I knew. It hurt, but I sang Same Script, Different Cast by Whitney Houston and Deborah Cox, and she cried until she drifted off to sleep.

And now? My heart is breaking, like hers did that night. But I don't have any letters, just the memories of his lies.

Life keeps throwing these damn pop quizzes, like some stubborn teacher who won't stop until I pass. And me? I'm the hard-headed student who thinks she can ace it just because a man shows up and plays nice for a semester.

I knew better, and I didn't want to face it because those lies felt so damn good in the moment. All because he "took care of me". Moments gone. No more cheating ass cheaters for me, I don't care how long your money is.

CHAPTER TWENTY-FOUR – DATING WOES

I push through what feels like a decade's worth of raggedy dates and tragic comedy routines disguised as men. It's April 2011, and it hasn't even been a year since I broke things off with Stephen, but who's counting?

As Marie and I walk into the beauty supply store, I catch the security guard doing a slow double take. I'm not in the mood for any "Hey, beautiful black Nubian queen" energy, so I keep it moving. I slide my bags across the counter for him to check.

"Hi, beautiful. Pick your head up; you're too gorgeous to be walking with your head down."

I can't quite tell if he's being for real or if he says this shit to everybody.

"Well, thank you, but I'm just trying not to trip and bust my ass. I'm clumsy like that."

We both have a good laugh.

I hook my arm through Marie's as I laugh and steer us into the aisles.

"Girrrl," Marie whispers a few minutes later, eyes wide, chin tilting behind me. "Ain't that your security guard?"

I glance back, and sure enough, here comes Mr. Security rolling through on one of those little electric scooters. He's slow enough to be creepy, but fast enough to keep up, watching us like we just shoved lace front wigs into our purses.

I side-eye him and give a slight grin and head nod to let him know I see him.

"Lord… girl, what is this man up to?"

We laugh and keep shopping as we pretend not to notice him doing lazy loops around the store.

At checkout, we pay for our stuff, grab the receipt, and head to reclaim our bags. That's when he leans over the counter.

"Love, can I tell you something?"

My eyebrow raises as I try to back up a little. I glance at Marie, who is already chewing her lip, so she doesn't laugh out loud.

I look at him with a nervous anticipation. "Sure?"

"You're my future wife," he says.

"Your future wife? Oh, boy, we skipping all the middle parts, huh?"

"It sounds crazy, I know, but listen, you're my wife. I know you are. I'm meant for you, and you're meant for me. God told me that when I saw you."

"Oh, God just told you that?"

I stare at him with a blank expression.

Marie stands behind him mouthing, *bitch, no*, as he keeps going with his TED Talk that I sure as hell didn't ask for.

"What's up with the scar on your face?" he says, pointing at my cheek.

"Don't ask." I swat the air like I just killed the question. I really don't feel like the reaction right now.

"Okayyy, well, here, I have something to give you."

He reaches down to his pant pocket, and I can't hide the confusion on my face.

"Uhhh... okayyy? What is it?"

Mr. Security unhooks a key from his key chain, and I'm even more confused as I watch this unfold. Why do I attract guys like this?

He grabs my hand, flips it over, and places the key in my palm. Then, like this is a rom-com instead of a red flag festival, he scribbles an address on the back of a coupon and slides that over too.

"Yes, it's real," he says, eyes focused on me, "and here's my phone number. I want you to text me right now before you leave so I can have yours."

Sir. This is a beauty supply store, not a speed dating event. But okay, go off.

I pull up my Google Voice app and send a quick "Hey" just to get this over with. There's no way I'm giving him my real number. Next thing you know, I'll have him lurking outside my apartment on that little scooter.

"My name is Terry Brown, short for Terrence. Look me up; do your background work. I'm a well-known entrepreneur, I'm safe. I want to take you on a date because, like I said, you're my wife. That's the key and address to our house, and you can stop by anytime you want."

I blink at him, my face doing all the math.

"Okay, Terry... sooo... how many extra keys do you got on that key chain to just be passing them out to random women?"

"It's not even like that...But!" he says as he throws up one finger, "I'm gonna need you to pick me up for our date because I don't have a car."

"Ohhh, you don't have a car?"

"Nah, wifey, I'm working on it."

I bite back a laugh.

"Well, Terry, I'm looking forward to that date," Lying my ass off.

"But I gotta go because my friend's husband is waiting for her." Another lie! "Call ya later, future husband!"

I force a smile, grab Marie's hand, and damn near sprint for the door.

The second we hit the car; we both let out a synchronized scream.

Marie slaps the dashboard, gasping for air, and I'm doubled over in the passenger seat like my ribs are about to crack.

"Girl! Did that man just give you a house key and tell you to pick him up?" She wheezes.

"Yes! And an address to a place I bet he doesn't even pay rent at!"

I grab the key out of my pocket and throw it in the cup holder, disgusted.

"Who gives a stranger a key to their place? Girl, why does this shit happen to me?"

Marie laughs so hard, she's almost sitting on the floor of the car.

"Saliya, you better hope that ain't a trap house."

"Pssh, we aren't even about to find out! I don't care if it was a damn henhouse! I'm not about to be the next headline: Local Woman Slain by Security Guard on Scooter. No ma'am!"

We sit there for a second, trying to calm down, but the image of him rolling up in that electric scooter like Paul Blart: Mall Husband, sends us into another fit.

"Ohhh, Saliya! Let's go to the address and see if the key works?"

I hit the brakes before I can pull off all the way.

"Absofuckinglutely not! Girl, this is the stuff that gets you on First 48. I come in for some edge control and leave engaged to a psychopath."

I glance over my shoulder as I put the car in drive again before the scooter comes flying through the parking lot.

Dating was supposed to be fun again. Fresh start, clean slate. But every man I meet reminds me why I'm single.

There was the guy whose mother chased me out of karaoke for my number. Only for me to climb into a trash-filled car on our one and only date. Then I quickly realized he was more interested in the men at the pool hall than my sexy ass outfit. Baby, I almost got the dude's number for my boy.

Then came Mr. "no washcloth, just hands", no thank you, I enjoy having bacteria free, dead skin cell free skin.

And then there was the man who didn't even make it to a first date, because in less than five hours he went from "hey beautiful" to Costco-sample-quality dick promos.
Dick and balls flying at my screen like a semi-

automatic Nerf gun.
Blocked, blocked, blocked again.

None of those tragedies beat the cherry on top of the sundae: **the social services lobby meeting.**

I'm at the social services building, trying to find a babysitter so my auntie can finally take a breath. I'm minding my business, filling out paperwork, when somebody walks in and my spirit taps me on the shoulder.

It's Rashid.

High-school 'stole his mama's car so we can take a joyride' Rashid.
Ninth-grade summer Rashid.
'One kiss and his breath could kill a houseplant' Rashid, that Rashid.

I should've run in the opposite direction, but no, hopeless romantic me thinks the universe is doing a soft reset. *Won't He do it.*
We exchange numbers. I'm thinking maybe God is in the neighborhood.

We talk a lot, but we never go out. He pulls up once, we chill, nothing happens, and that's that. No pressure. No spark. Just *talking.*

I'm thinking, *eh, okay, no rush*.

Life keeps life-ing, and I finally find a babysitter; a sweet woman with three or four kids of her own.

About a month goes by, and the kids adore her.
One day, I show up to get them with my hair freshly braided; by me, thank you very much.

"Ohhh, Saliya, your hair is so pretty! You think you could do mine?"

Of course I can. I'm a mother. A hustler. A woman of many trades.

She comes over, I'm braiding her hair, and we agree we have to stop at 3 p.m. because the buses won't wait for anyone. We have to get these kids.

We're talking about school. I tell her I went to Heritage High School.

She goes, "Oh! You might know my fiancé."

I laugh. "Girl, maybe. I was quiet."

Then she says his name.

"His name is Rashid."

And my armpits light up like a smoke alarm.

I'm sitting there with a comb in my hand, trying not to pass out.

I say, as calmly as I can,
"Oh yeah… I know Rashid. We dated briefly in high school. Nothing serious."

Inside, I'm screaming:
THE MAN WHO'S BEEN TEXTING ME EVERY DAY LIVES IN YOUR HOUSE? YOUR FIANCÉ??

She keeps talking…
Meanwhile I'm realizing I've been dropping my kids off at THIS woman's home for a whole month. And this man has been upstairs like a fraudulent ghost.

Mid-braid, I pick up my phone and text him:
"You know we're done talking, right."

No explanation. No punctuation gymnastics. Just closure.

At 3 p.m., she says, "I gotta get the baby off the bus. You wanna come finish my hair at my house?"

Oh, I ABSOLUTELY want to go to that house. DAMN RIGHT!

We pack up, get my kid off the bus, and head over.

I'm in her living room now, braiding the hair of a woman who trusts me more than she should trust the man she sleeps next to.

Then I hear footsteps on the stairs, and a satisfied grin spreads across my face like I'm the Grinch and its Christmas Eve.

He walks down.

No eye contact.

He looks like guilt wearing basketball shorts, and I'm still in disbelief that the good lord saw fit for me to be in this moment.

"Babe, don't be rude! Say hi! You and Saliya went to high school together!"

I look right at him.
"Yeah, don't be rude. Hey, Rashid."

He mumbles, "What's up," and keeps walking like the floor is suddenly fascinating.

After that? Blocked. Deleted. Forgotten like last season's shoes.

I mean, If this was the dating pool, hope was lost. But then I had some excitement.

55.

No name, just 55, and 55 swooped in so smoothly. He came in with consistent conversation for six months, no dates, no begging, and very attentive and intriguing. Never even mentioned sex, and that got my attention.

When we finally met up for Mexican and margaritas (my love language, and no, I will never part with it), he was everything. Great conversation. Hug reciprocated. And when he walked me to my car and pulled me in with that lower back grab?

Yeah… I knew right then I was gonna give this man some. Don't judge me; my radar for good dick is deadly accurate.

Two weeks later, we had another date planned, but I called him after my friend's birthday party earlier that day. It ran later than we had planned.

"Hey love, can we ditch the date and watch movies? I'm exhausted."

55 agreed without hesitation. When I got there, this man's house was decorated to the gods. Plants. Red and black décor. Bar set-up like he hosted high-end wine tastings. Plush couch I could've disappeared into.

He asked if I wanted a glass of wine. Then he pulled out my favorite; Roscato. I know, I knowww. It's so basic. But it's got me in a chokehold.

I smiled, knowing exactly what was about to happen.

A couple of hours of "trying" to watch movies turned into talking, and talking turned into him inviting me to "go lay down in the back, babe, you look like you're getting tired."

His only rule? "I just gotta let you know, no clothes in my bed. Not even socks."

Now, Sir…

I walked back there naked before he could even finish his sentence, pulling off clothes, leaving a trail for him to follow. As soon as I step in the room, he already has Barry White playing. *Okay, fitting, I guess.*

That night was… dangerous. Pleasure on loop. It was a neck grabbing, booty smacking, choked up good time. When I got home the next morning, I had hickies on my ankles, chest, and thighs. Ankles!!!

And that's exactly why I texted him, "We will not be seeing each other again." Because I'm not about to be out here losing my dignity, and my mind, behind a 55-year-old with good dick. BLOCKED.

I smiled for two weeks every time I looked at those fading hickies, just thinking about that time that was had! Self-preservation. It's all about self-preservation, ladies. But 55 sure was fun.

CHAPTER TWENTY-FIVE – THE ILLUSION

It's June 2012. Life hasn't been handing me too many lemons lately, and I'm thankful for that.

Tonight, I'm doing my usual karaoke night with my cousin, her boyfriend, and his friend Anthony. I keep it casual but cute on purpose, presentable but not purchasable, that's my motto. We're all having a good time, then Anthony leans in.

"What's up, Saliya? I was about to ask you to shoot a game of pool with me. But first, can I just say… you are beautiful. And your skin? Whew. That skin tone is perfect."

For a second, I just stand there, amused, and a little caught off guard.

"Well, Anthony, I wasn't expecting that, but you just made my evening. Thank you."

My breathing picks up just enough for me to notice, and that rush of heat in my body tells me all I need to know. There's chemistry.

Lordy, girl calm the fuck down. What is wrong with you?

Anthony stands about 5'8", lean with cut muscles, and long cornrowed locs all the way down his back.

My eyes take the scenic route, starting at his shoes and working their way up.
And honestly? Sometimes I think Momma accidentally birthed two boys, because the way I objectify men sometimes can be low-key disrespectful.

"Hmph, let's play that game, Anthony. I'd love that."

He catches me in the act, laughing like he knows exactly what that once-over means, flashing a smile that could ruin a woman's life in the best way. My mind drifts into a whole daydream; we're having the most insane, up-against-the-wall kind of sex in my living room.

"Break. Saliya! Break!"

Anthony's voice grabs my attention.

"Girl, you nasty," I say to myself under my breath as I grab my pool stick.

His head whips around, confused.

"Excuse me?"

I stammer as I try to fix it quickly.

"More! More karaoke?"

We both laugh and start our round of pool.

It ends up feeling like a double date, but without all the deep "tell me your childhood trauma" type conversations. We just enjoy each other's company with lots of eye contact, laughing at terrible renditions of "Endless Love."

From that night on, we were together. Every night. The friendship turned into a relationship, and that relationship bloomed for two years. There's something about Anthony that makes me feel safe in a way I never knew I needed.

It's the complete opposite of the chaos I had in my marriage, and even with Stephen. It's deeper than what I had with Jacoby, and more intimate than Mr. Bankman.

Okay, that's enough flipping through my dating Rolodex.

Anthony's love for music and the way he respects women has me locked in. He's so aware of me, my safety, and my emotions, sometimes staring right through me. It's comforting.

Most nights I meet him at the studio, and let me tell you, what a time to be alive. This night is no different. My girls are fast asleep at my mom's house, and she makes sure I get my "me" time.

That's when I feel the pulse of my freedom. I throw on the tiniest bit of clothing I can get away with; tonight it's an oversized T-shirt that hits my knees, nothing underneath but a whisper of perfume, and some heels.

I pull up to the studio with Rihanna's "S&M" blasting, and strut up to the "Stu," as he calls it. Anthony hears my knock and opens the door with that half-smile that always makes me forget whatever was weighing me down.

The room is low-lit, glowing softly from the wall lights and the little blinking buttons on his equipment. The air is thick with the scent of incense, sandalwood, and secrets.

His eyes slide down to my shoes and back up to my face.

"Damn. Oh, you really tryna mess up my concentration tonight?"

I laugh as I brush my shoulder against his chest, and I step inside.

"Not at all. Well... I mean, maybe. Depends on how good this beat is."

I plop down on the couch, tuck my legs under me, rest my chin on my hand, and I watch him move around the room like it's part of him. Fingers flying over his laptop, twisting knobs, and sliding buttons until something locks into place.

"I love watching you in your element. You glow. Did you know that?"

He glances over his shoulder and smirks. "I glow, huh? Baby girl, that's all you. I been meaning to ask you, what's up with this scar under your eye?"

I shake my head and lean forward; my hands rest on his knees.

"Fell when I was 4, cracked my face on a toilet. Blood. Stitches. Trauma. Poem!"

He laughs and throws up his hands in surrender. "You got it, beautiful, go right ahead."

I laugh and clear my throat.

Funny the many times into someone's eyes I've looked,

Yet never have I once become lost,

Never so speechless had I been or rare a moment placed upon me.

Never so profound a feeling of relief.

So brief a moment has left a print in my heart,

As though reassuring, worry not and fear not.

You're safe here…

Still, on my way I must go.

Funny the many times I've fallen, never has a fall been so sweet.

Never so significant has been a timing, so beautiful an artless place,

Very fascinating was the figure, a familiar touch, harmless and true.

I have fallen in love.

There's silence, and he turns back to the screen. "Wow. You always say the right stuff when I'm not recording it. Chill with that. Girl, that was beautiful."

He's like the most breathtaking sunrise, the kind you don't just watch... you feel. And I felt it on the couch, on the floor, across the keyboards. I felt it everywhere that night.

CHAPTER TWENTY-SIX – TURN THE BEAT DOWN

It's September, and for his birthday this year, I want to make him feel special.

I put together a gift basket with all his favorites; his go-to snacks, an upgraded mic for the Stu, and a personalized journal for his music notes. I'm cooking his favorite dinner: grilled salmon, garlic mashed potatoes, and roasted asparagus.

Time is not on my side, and my nerves and foggy brain really start to show their ass, and so I give him a call. I want everything perfect, and I want to make sure he has no clue what I'm up to.

"Hey Anthony, when do you think you'll be over today?"

"Hey love, I'm gonna wrap up here at the studio in a couple of hours. I'll be over around 7 p.m."

Two hours. I've got two hours, but I wait to cook so everything will be hot when he walks in.

"Okay. I'll see you then, and you be safe out there. I love you."

It rolls off my tongue like butter. My heart's racing as I light the candles, pour the wine, and take one last look in the mirror.

Girl you look good!

Tonight is going to be unforgettable.

Somewhere between fluffing the pillows and adjusting the silverware, time slips through my fingers, and 7 p.m. becomes 8 p.m. He's probably caught up at the Stu or his mom's house now.

I plate his food on my best dish, drizzle sauce, and climb into bed to wait. When I call him, though, no answer, and so I send a text, but I don't get a reply.

"Okay, bitch… NOW we can get mad,"

I sit down and my eyelids betray me. I drift off with him on my mind.

A hard knock at the door jolts me awake, and I glance at the clock before rushing over.

9:17 p.m.

The smell of alcohol greets me before his slurred words do.

"Anthony... are you drunk?"

"Saliya, baby, I went out with the boys for my birthday, and I'm so sorry I'm late. But yes, I had a few drinks,"

He sways in the doorway, testing every ounce of my patience.

"I'm so tired," he says, as he kicks off his shoes.

"Mmm! It's smell good, baby, you cooked? Can you just wrap my plate up for me? I'm so tired."

Wait a second. Did he just show up late, drunk, and dismiss the dinner I sweated my hair out to cook? But my old habit of being agreeable taps me on the shoulder again, whispering.

Don't start a fight it's his day.

"Okay, lay down, babe."

I watch as he stumbles toward my room, collapsing onto the bed without a second thought.

I crawl into my recliner with the television on mute, as I try to swallow the feeling that something is wrong. Out of the corner of my eye, his phone lights up on the armrest where he placed it. I glance at him before my gaze darts back to the phone.

"No password. Free game!" I say it just above a whisper just to test the depth of his sleep.

He doesn't move.

I walk softly over to the phone, trying to mentally prepare for what I might see. I pick up the phone and start scrolling… and what I find…

You've been talking to five different women. FIVE.

I laugh quietly, manically.

"Is this my karma? It has to be."

I read each text message thread carefully. My thumb hovers over a recent conversation with a woman named Tiffany, and my stomach turns as I scroll through their texts.

"Hey love, I hope you made it to your mom's safely. Was the dinner good? I know the dessert was amazing."

The emojis, the boldness. THE FUCKING AUDACITY of this man. My blood runs cold. So, this is where he was before he stumbled into my house, drunk and useless.

I sit the phone down where it was, with sweaty hands, and I stare at the ceiling, blinking back tears. I don't know whether to scream, cry, or throw something at his damn head.

Instead, I sit there until the sun rises, until my thoughts quiet into numb resignation.

"No rest for the weary, I guess," I whisper as I cut my eyes at him. I shove his shoulder to wake him up so that I can leave for work.

I kiss Anthony goodbye like nothing is wrong. I got something sweet for your ass.

"Have a good day, babe," I say in the sweetest voice I can find.

He smiles sleepily.

"You too, love."

When I get into my car, the tears flow, and when I arrive at work, I park in the back of the parking lot where no one can see me. I sit in the car, gripping the steering wheel as sobs wrack my body. I haven't felt like this in a while. It's so unexpected, and I'm sick of saying *I never thought it would be him.*

"Okay, Saliya. Shake this shit off. Shake it off, go into this job, and hold it together."

The walk into work feels bitter, cold, but I try to appear as if nothing happened, like my heart isn't in pieces. By lunch I can't hold it anymore and I tell my work besties everything. You better believe they are here for the tea.

"He was with some girl named Tiffany last night and had the nerve to come straight to my place afterwards and go to sleep. And he's been texting all these other women!"

Mariya's face matches my disgust.

"Oh, hell no. We're not letting that slide."

"Aye, I need y'all to do me a favor," I say, scowling, because a petty little plan is forming.

"What's up, Saliya?"

They all chime in, which makes me laugh despite my feelings.

"I'm giving each of you one of these numbers. Call them and tell them Anthony's a dirty-ass dog. Tell them he's been playing them and make it bad. Like 'ruin-his-day' bad."

Mariya grins, eyes lighting up like it's Christmas. "Oh, I'm on this. I love a good game of go low, and I'll go lower." Within an hour, the calls are done.

"Handled!" Mariya is the first one done, and she wears her smirk proudly. "One of those chicks even cried. Like, girl, get your life together. I just told you your man's a whore," she laughs.

I laugh, but it's hollow, a cover. "Thanks, y'all. I appreciate it."

"You good, Saliya?"

"Mariya, girl, I don't know. I just... needed them to know, ya know? But now what? He's still a liar, and I'm still a sad ass mess."

When I clock out, I sit in my car staring at my phone until I finally dial his number. I force my voice to sound as normal as possible. "Anthony, hey boo,"

"Saliya, hey baby. What's up?"

...but there's something off in his tone. Did my plan work?

"Hmmm, is everything okay? You sound upset."

"Yeah, just a crazy day. A little stressed, but I'll be okay, baby girl, thanks for noticing."

"Well, um, some lady called me today. Talking wild, said you ain't shit and that you have a girlfriend."

The silence on his end says everything, but I wait anyway.

"I don't know what that was about, but I promise I'm not messing with anyone else," he says with confidence.

"Okay, Anthony. If you say so."

I feel better for a second because I know I accomplished my mission, but I'm still hurt.

Over time, the calls get fewer, shorter, colder, and so I just go with the flow. Not like I'm looking for anyone else. But a month later, my phone rings, and it's an unfamiliar number. One not saved in my phone.

"Hello?" I say as I wonder who's voice is going to be on the other end.

"Hey babe, it's Anthony."

"Uh... hey, Anthony. What's up with the new number?"

He pauses.

"Hey, Saliya, I just called to tell you our relationship isn't really going in the direction I want. I have to call it quits."

I blink a few times, stunned but not shocked.

"Wow, Really, Anthony? I know It's been awkward since your birthday, but what's this shit you saying now?"

"Look, I can't explain, sorry, I just... can't do it anymore. I wish I could go into detail, baby girl, but right now I can't."

My body heats up before I have a chance to think about what I want to say next.

"You know what, Anthony? Keep the apology. And if you can't explain now, don't bother explaining later, I'm good!"

I hang up before he can say another word. I scroll to his name, hit block, and let his ass go, along with two and a half years of my life. Can I get through two years without being screwed over?

Outside of Stephen, I had never felt so strongly about someone being my person. There has gotta be a two-year hold on my love life.

CHAPTER TWENTY-SEVEN – THE SPARK THAT NEVER CAME BACK

Another two years fly by, not because time is kind, but because I am too busy putting the pieces of my life and heart together to notice it passing. It's now June 2014, and I'm focused.

My daughters are thriving; 10, 8, and 6 years old. Christina will be 7 in August. We dance in the kitchen most evenings to '90s R&B, trying new recipes, laughing, and building routines that make our little apartment feel like home.

We have movie nights on Fridays, store runs we don't need, but enjoy, and impromptu hugs from tiny arms that remind me I'm doing something right.

Their father? Still absent, and behind in child support. I make peace with the pieces because I don't want to give life to situations that disappoint me.

Professionally, I'm in my bag managing a tire production facility. It's not champagne and roses, but there's beauty in it. The rumbling of the machines, the smell of rubber and oil, the way my crew checks in with me before making a big move. I've got grease under my nails and pride in my chest because I earned this.

My edges are moisturized, and my credit is healthy. What more can a girl ask for?

That's when he pops back up. Jacoby. Yes, Jacoby.
My sinful, sinful downfall from when I decided to be an adulteress, no, adulterer; hell, BOTH. I was out here embarrassing myself.

Oh shit… this man done found me on social media. And I finally know his last name.
Jacoby Travis: What's up stranger.

I guess this is the male version of "hey big head."
Is social media the new way to track people down? Damn, I need an alias…
But…my excitement leads to curiosity.

A whole fantasy blooms in the notification bubble; us, older now, wiser, healed. Maybe this time the timing is right, and we'll choose each other.

After some back-and-forth, I tell him I'll stop by after my girls' night. We let the conversation rest there and exchange numbers.

A few drinks later, I pull up to his place. I need to sit down for a second anyway, so I park and take a breath before getting out. Jacoby is already at the end of the driveway, waiting.

He pulls me into a hug and, man, he hasn't aged at all. "Damn, Saliya, you look good as hell."

"You don't look too bad yourself," I say, as I step inside the house. "I can't even lie… I think about you a lot."

His eyes spark; familiar, dangerously soft. "I knew it," he smirks. "You always been the one that got away."

I roll my eyes because that line is just so corny to me, but my smile gives me away. "Boy, please."

We sit in the living room like two people revisiting an old fire hazard.

"How many kids you got now?" he asks, leaning back like he belongs in the moment.

"Three," I say. "Nicole's eleven. Had her in 2004."

He pauses. The air shifts.

"2004? So… is there any chance—"

"No."
My answer sprints out before he finishes.

He lifts his hands and laughs lightly. "My bad, my bad. Just needed to ask. Fair enough."

"So," he says, licking his lips a little too slow, "you tryna pick up where we left off? See what this could be again?"

I inhale.
"I mean... things in my life are flowing right now. My girls are good, my job is good, and I'm good. If anything happens between us, I want it to be slow. Real slow. I'm not trying to disrupt what's finally working."

He stands, steps closer, tilts my chin like old times.
"Slow?" he murmurs. "Maybe I can convince you otherwise."

Before I can protest, he leans down and kisses me and Lord...Why did he do that? I swear to God, I feel NOTHING. Actually, I'm disgusted. No spark, no flutter, no warmth, just lips. Sloppy and wet.

UGHHHHHHHH.

Why is his tongue sloshing around like he forgot how to kiss? Or maybe I just forgot how to receive one.

Is this how he kissed back then? I'm appalled at my damn self if I found this acceptable.

There's so much slob on my lips I want to gag. I think he's actually trying to swallow my whole face. I pull back, wipe my mouth with my shirt, and blink several times in pure "what the fuck was that."

I pat his chest, push him back slightly, and I reach for my bag. "Great kiss, Jacoby... wow. As good as that kiss was, friend, I kinda gotta get back home to the kids."

I see the heartbreak on his face; like he had the same thought I had, before that kiss that came from the depths of hell.

I turn around, and I run. I run away. I don't look back. No hug goodbye.

A few days later, he texts me again asking for a DNA test, saying Nicole might be his.

I have to laugh. Not mean, just done. "Jacoby, that's not even physically possible.

Nicole is very clearly her father's child. He already took me down this road."

He never responds. And that's it.

Every now and then, he pops up in my "People You May Know," his little digital wave. His little, "I see you."

Sometimes my mind wanders to a world where we ended up together. A world where the timing made sense and we lived happily ever after like the version of us I used to fantasize about.

But the truth is… I'm happy I'm not her anymore. The spark didn't die. I just outgrew that shit.

And for that, for the woman I am now, for the peace I didn't have back then, I'm thankful.

Sometimes I think God just tests me; *Let's see if she still fallin' for the same type…*

Well…

CHAPTER TWENTY-EIGHT – YOU WIN SOME

When HR tells my coworker and me to run and grab lunch for the crew, I don't think twice. "Aiight, Saliya, bring yo' ass on out here, girl. We gotta get this food."

I stop in my tracks, put my hand on the door, and tilt my head just enough to give Jameson the mama side-eye. "Uh… who do you think you talkin' to like that?"

He grins like he's been waiting all day to poke the bear. "Girl, come on here before I pull off!" Dimples deep, eyes daring me to keep playing.

We've talked in my office nearly every day for years, but today… something's different. Maybe it's been too long since I've looked at anybody with fresh eyes. Or maybe I'm just noticing details I used to overlook.

Either way, I tuck the thought in the back of my mind. Some things are better left to marinate. I lean on the doorframe, trying to play it cool. "You just don't kidnap me, Jameson, okay? You seem a little off. I gotta keep my eye on you."

Mmm. Those damn dimples flash again.

"Watch me, but don't tempt me."

I roll my eyes, but a smirk sneaks in before I can catch it, and I hate that I don't hate it. It's that mix of charm and trouble I should know better than to entertain. But here I am, already feeling the pull, like my brain's whispering, *this one could be different.*

That night, while I'm folding laundry and minding my business, I catch myself smiling again. Over that damn Jameson. I shake my head, toss a shirt into the pile, and reach for my phone.

Nope, not doing it.

I toss it onto the couch.

Two seconds later, I'm picking it back up like I didn't just have that whole "we're not doing this" conversation with myself.

"Girl... send the damn text," I say to give myself the nudge I need.

Me: Hey, Jameson.

Message sent.

Now I'm checking my phone every thirty seconds like a middle schooler waiting on a crush, and I am not okay. The text chime hits sooner than I expect.

Jameson: Hey cutie, what's up?

I pause. Think for maybe half a second. Hmmm, he called me cute again.

Me: Nothing much, Jameson. You wanna come over and watch a movie?

Okay, maybe it is forward. But the kids are gone for the summer, and I've got nothing but time to make questionable decisions. My thumb hovers over "send" longer than I'd like to admit before I hit it.

He replies almost instantly.

Jameson: Yeah, I'm takin' the bike out later, so I'll swing by.

No emoji. No "lol." Just smooth, casual, and effortless. Ugh, I hate that shit. He's building up suspense that I'm pulling for, but not ready for.

When he arrives a little after eight, my favorite series is already playing, and the lights are dimmed just enough to feel warm and not desperate. He steps in with his motorcycle helmet tucked under one arm, cologne hitting in all the right ways.

"So… really, Saliya? Why you call me over here?" he says, eyebrow raised with a puzzled smile. "I'm just saying that text was very random."

I lean against the counter with my arms folded, giving him my best you asked for it grin. "Well, maybe I'm attracted to you, just a little." I pinch my fingers together. "That's why I told you to come over. But I'm not looking for a relationship. I've been through some things, and I'm still figuring my shit out. I just want the company."

He studies me for a moment, nodding like he's taking mental notes, then walks to the couch, setting his helmet on the table. "Okay, I can respect that."

I sit next to him, and he slides closer. Not in a way that makes me pull back, but close enough that I can feel it; that quiet sincerity you don't have to guess about.

"But just so you know, I'm interested in you too, real talk," he says. "You got this fire… and a calm at the same time. I like both. But what the fuck happened to your face? Looks like that shit hurt."

My eyes narrow, and I blink at him with a straight face. "Four years old. Face. Toilet. Stitches."

"Damn! The *toilet*? Shit, you lucky you didn't drown."

I stare, blankly. "...Don't."

He shrugs. "Aight, chill, I was just sayin'."

That night, we don't cross any lines. We talk, we laugh, and somewhere between swapping stories and sharing a blanket, we fall asleep on opposite ends of the couch. And just like that... It starts.

CHAPTER TWENTY-NINE – THE SMOKE CLEARS

The next few weeks are a blur; hot and heavy, equal parts laughter, sex, and food. I love it here. No pressure, no timelines.

"Hey, Saliya, I'm working in North Carolina this week, so I won't be able to see you." His voice drops like he hates saying it.

"Wow," I say, matching his tone. "I was really looking forward to it, Jameson. When do you think you'll be home?"

"Won't be home until Saturday, Saliya, I'm sorry." I can hear him moving around, the rustle of bags, and the thud of a car door shuts him into work mode.

There's a pause. A flicker of longing hits me in a way I don't want to name yet. "Well… guess I'll have to take a road trip to North Carolina tomorrow, huh?" I say, teasing him.

But he doesn't laugh with me. "Do that," he says.

Okay, now he's challenging me. Did he mean that? My heart stumbles a little. "I mean, the kids are gone for the summer, so don't dare me," I say, just waiting on his word to jump.

"Dare," he says right back, in a serious tone.

We laugh, but there's something else in it, a push, a test, a pull I decide not to fight. "Hmph, I'll see you Thursday, and I can't wait."

When we hang up, I'm already pulling up the dealership website to schedule an oil change and tire rotation. I won't be stranded on the side of the road.

When I hit the road, it's like slipping into a familiar version of myself. There's something about driving that puts me in the calmest space. The sound of tires on asphalt, the blur of green and blue outside my window, the sun playing peek-a-boo, in and out of the trees. It's therapy on four wheels.

I roll the windows down just enough to let the wind kiss my face without turning my braids into a bird's nest. Eryn Allen Kane's Aviary: Act II is on repeat, and I'm singing like the steering wheel is my mic. "Now and Then" hits different, like it's peeling back layers I didn't even know were loose.

It's tender and heavy all at once, making me think about how quickly moments turn into memories. How easy it is to miss what's slipping away until it's already gone. I can't help wondering if I'm driving toward something real... or something I just want to be real.

Marie keeps me company for most of the five hours, our conversation making the trip fly. My nerves are shot by the time I pull into the hotel lot where Jameson's crew is staying. I'm falling fast, and I don't care if it's quicksand.

But there he is. Big, beautiful smile, already at the lobby door, walking toward my car like he's been waiting all day. We settle in; the room carrying that mix of his cologne and hotel disinfectant. I unpack, pulling out a little surprise, a drinking game for couples. Light, flirty, nothing too serious. He doesn't drink, but I do, and hey... he can reap the benefits of whatever tipsy generosity follows.

"Jameson, I got a game I wanna play."

I wave the box in the air like it's a prize on The Price is Right. "It's one of those 'get to know you' games. Truth or drink, but with cards." I toss in a wink.

His expression changes to disgust in an instant. "Oh, nah. I don't play shit like that, I mean, unless you tryna learn something you really don't wanna find out," he says, "I don't play games."

The bluntness makes me sit up a little straighter without even realizing it. He lets out this short, awkward laugh, like he's trying to soften the hit but not really.

"Ohhh-kayyy…"

I set the box down gently on the dresser, like it might go off if I drop it.

"Damn, Jameson, not even one card?"

He shrugs, already turning toward the mini fridge. "Nah, for real. Games like that start arguments. People dig, and I ain't in the mood to be a science project tonight."

I nod slowly, still smiling, but my mind's moving faster than my mouth because that was… unexpected.

I'm not trying to dissect him, just connect with him, but the way he shut it down feels like a closed door I wasn't even knocking that hard on. And if I'm honest, I can't ignore it. I tuck that moment into my mental pocket, the way women do when something doesn't sit quite right. But is it outright wrong?

Note to self: Maybe he doesn't like emotional depth? Bet. Give the man some grace...for now.

We end the night cuddling with a movie, and I settle for that quality time. I let my body sink into his, grateful for the warmth and the quiet.
But even with my head on his chest, feeling the steady beat of his heart, my eyes drift toward the box on the dresser. Unopened. Unwanted.

Part of me wants to brush it off as nothing. But another part, the quieter, wiser part, knows that sometimes, the things we laugh off are the things that matter most.

Life with Jameson just... continues. No big announcement, no defining moment, he folds into my days like he's always been there. That summer, while the kids are gone, he becomes part of my routine without me even realizing it. Mornings blur into evenings with him. I ride behind him on his motorcycle, my arms locked around his waist, wind in my face, feeling like I'm in a music video I don't want to end.

By September, I'm cooking breakfast at his place on weekends; cheesy scrambled eggs, buttery toast, and hot coffee exactly how he likes it. He takes me out for Mexican and margaritas often, and we linger for hours, talking about everything and nothing at the same time.

It's December 2014, and we're six months in; we've got a rhythm. No need to talk about who grabs the road trip snacks or who picks the podcast. I drive because it's my thing, and his playlists in time become mine. I catch myself humming Bazzi's song Beautiful in the kitchen while I wash dishes, scrolling through old texts just to hear his laugh in my head.

One afternoon, he takes me to this hole-in-the-wall Jamaican spot tucked in a strip plaza I've driven past a hundred times. One bite of that oxtail, and I'm ready to file a complaint against every chain restaurant I've ever supported. Because this shit is good.

Our nights? Incredible. I forget the pain of our shallow relationship in tangled sheets, jokes, and kisses. But it's the ease that pulls me in; the way he wants me to rub his stomach because that's what his mother used to do, and the way he lets me nurture.

His eyes tell a story he hasn't learned to tell himself. A story of sadness I can't look away from. That's when I realize I love him.

Still… sometimes, when he's asleep and I'm staring at the ceiling, I wonder if what we have is real, or if it's just the perfect escape from what we've both survived, his grief, my pain.

Comfort can trick you like that. It lulls you into ignoring the signs, the missed call here and there, the delayed text on Monday that's fine by Tuesday, the last-minute "dealing with some stuff." The distance that makes my stomach turn, followed up with a closeness that makes me forget. I brush it off; we're adults, life happens.

But does it?

For the New Year, we make an impromptu trip to Washington, D.C., and its perfect; just us for three days in a fancy hotel. I'm buzzing with excitement, dragging my suitcase through the lobby.

"Babe, get the door."

Like clockwork, I nudge him with my elbow when he forgets. He smirks, jogs ahead, and pulls it open with an exaggerated bow. I roll my eyes, but I still laugh. I love the idea of going to sleep and waking up together, no rush, no interruptions.

The only hiccup is my overeating. My stomach protests instantly. I'm doubled over in the bathroom, groaning, and yell through the door.

"If you hear me die in here, tell my kids I love them!"

He cracks up from the bed as I hit play on my playlist from my phone, my attempt to drown out the embarrassment. But the first song that plays is I Wanna Rock by Luke. Not what I needed, but the good Lord always sees fit.

"Don't play; you know you're greedy, and really! Saliya? That song?" He says as I cover my face, mortified, but eventually I laugh too.

The best part comes on our last day. We stumble across a pair of electric scooters and take off, weaving through the streets like kids. My hair whips in the chilly wind, and our laughter echoes against the buildings.

"If I win, you gotta kiss my ass!" I shout, pushing the throttle.

He zooms past me.

"Oh, I was gonna do that anyway," he says, grinning like he already knows he's going to win. It's picture-perfect, a memory burned into me like sunlight.

CHAPTER THIRTY – WHO YOU ARE

By February 2015, life keeps rolling forward and we're on another adventure; a road trip to see his family. I love road trips. Windows down, music loud enough to feel it in my chest, snacks in the cup holder. Jameson leans back in the passenger seat, hat low, legs stretched out.

He deserves a rest; he's on the road for work every week. I glance at him, then back at the road, and smile. I don't mind driving. With him next to me, I feel like we could go anywhere.

We pull into the gas station. I park, waiting, because this part isn't my job. He'll pump. He'll clean the windshield; I can't see out of it when the sun hits at this time of day. But he doesn't move. Not even a twitch. Just scrolling on his phone like the gas is going to jump in the car by itself.

I wait one minute too long and then snatch my card and head inside to pay. When I come back, the passenger seat is empty. For a second, I think maybe he got it together, maybe he's finally pumping. But no, he's inside. I spot him through the glass doors, picking through candy.

Heat rises to my face. A couple of men at the next pump are watching, leaning on their cars, smirks curling. And here I am, pumping gas and stretching across the hood to wipe down the windshield while he's inside shopping. My hands shake with embarrassment, but I keep going.

He strolls out a minute too late with a drink and candy, looking satisfied. I slam the gas cap shut, get in the car, and drive. I don't say a word.

The silence hangs throughout the entire ride. By the time we pull up at his brother's house, he breaks first.
"What's your problem?" he says, with a confused look on his face. "You been acting funny the entire drive."

I cut the engine, staring straight ahead. "My problem is I pumped gas and cleaned the windshield in front of everybody. Then you walked out with Skittles like it was nothing."

He shakes his head. "Man, you always blowing stuff up. If you wanted me to pump, you could've just said so. Matter of fact, you could've sat your ass down until I came out the store, always moving too fast. You want the window clean, say it. I ain't a mind reader."

I whip my head toward him. "I need to say that? I need to ask you to pump the gas? Why I gotta tell you what to do and when, all the time like you don't know how to be a man?! How about you take the lead and use your words, Jameson? It's about me not standing out there looking stupid while my man is inside buying candy."

His jaw flexes. He throws his hands up.

"See, this is the thing; you always act like I'm wrong. Like whatever I do, it's not enough. You're always right! So yeah, maybe I don't think about it automatically, Saliya, because in my head, you got it. You always got it, and you gonna do what you want! And look at you, even when I try, you still mad."

His voice cracks, quick, and then he swallows it back down.

I soften, but not all the way. "Jameson, I do what I need to because I have to. But, when we're together, I need you to lean and not just let me, okay? I just, I can't explain it. It's so odd the way you move. I can't put my finger on it."

He looks away, jaw tight, eyes shining but locked down. And I realize it's not laziness that left me at that pump; it's the boy in him who never learned what showing up looks like.

We walk up to the porch, tension still thick. I plaster on a half-smile when his brother opens the door, but my body is anxious with everything unsaid.

Jameson flips the switch like it's nothing.

"Aye, what's up, man!"

He greets his brother and pulls him in for a hug and drops into the living room.

I trail behind, quiet, taking a seat on the edge of the couch. He tears open the Skittles bag and shakes a rainbow into his palm.

His brother laughs.

"Man, you still on them Skittles? You gon' rot your teeth out."

Jameson grins, tossing one in his mouth.

"Hey, at least the candy is sweet to me. She ain't been today."

He nods toward me with a sly smirk, the room chuckling with him.

I force a laugh, but my stomach knots. It's a joke, but not really.

He keeps going, aiming the spotlight at himself.

"Naw, but for real, she stay mad at me 'cause I'm not out here pumping gas like a NASCAR pit crew. I tell her, baby, you independent! You don't need me. Strong Black woman, right?"

He says it with that effortless charm, like it's all a game.

Everyone laughs again, but I hear the truth buried under his grin. This man just hides behind punchlines.

I let the laughter ripple around the room, but I don't join in this time. My smile is small, controlled. He wants me to be the punchline, but I'm not giving him that stage.

"Strong Black woman, huh?" I say lightly, leaning back on the couch. "I'm feeling more like the strong black man in this relationship these days."

The room goes quiet just long enough for my words to land. His brother smirks, holding in his laugh. "Damn, bro."

Jameson laughs, too loud, too quick, stuffing more Skittles in his mouth like he can chew up the moment. "Man, she always gotta get the last word." He shakes his head, but I see it; the flicker in his eyes, the truth he tries to bury under candy and charm. He heard me. He just doesn't know what to do with it.

By spring, I tell myself to let the "small stuff" slide. By summer, I'm swallowing my frustrations. Then one night in June, he casually mentions he's going to Paris.

"Oh, nice. Who's going?" I say, playing it cool.

He pauses.

"The kids," he says while he's brushing his teeth.

I lift a brow.

"Just you and… the kids?"

Another pause…

"Yea. Also, my daughter's mom and her boyfriend, oh, and some friends."

My mouth drops.

"Excuse me?"

"It's a family trip," he waves his hand like I'm overreacting. "She wants the kids to see their grandparents together," he says.

I laugh and hold my fingers to my temples. "Oh, so now y'all are flying to Paris as one big blended happy family? And I'm just twiddling my thumbs until you get back, and you want me here when you get back, right? I know we've just been dating a year, but what's the expectation for me to join these trips? Because, baby, this is just weird."

"Why are you making it a thing?" His voice spikes. "See, this is why I ain't even wanna tell you. You always—"

"What?!"

I'm on my feet before he can finish, anger radiating through me.

"I'm always what?!? Jameson, y'all went to Mexico, y'all went on a cruise, and now you're going to PARISSS!?! You didn't want to tell me because you know it sounds shady as fuck, Jameson! Don't flip this on me."

"Saliya, You acting like I'm taking her on some romantic getaway."

"Nah, I'm acting like your girlfriend, who's always waiting for y'all to get back, and I'm sick of biting my lip about it."

"Man, chill out with all this dramatic ass shit."

"Say one more word like that to me, Jameson. I dare you." I step closer. "You lie to me by omission. I'm not stupid. You give me crumbs of your life. We never have genuine conversations about us unless I'm upset and bring it up! And you expect me to be grateful? You want me to be quiet and shit. But, you know what? I was grateful. That's the wild part; I was so damn grateful for the scraps you threw my way."

"Ain't nobody throwing you scraps, chill Saliya."

"No? Then why am I still invisible to certain people? It's giving suspicion, Jameson, and the shit's weird!"

Silence. He says nothing.

"You can't answer that, can you?" I say, begging for an answer.

"Look," he exhales, finally softer. "I didn't want things to get messy. I was trying to protect what I had with you."

"By keeping me a secret, Jameson?"

"By not rushing it, Saliya! Damn!" he snaps back.

"You know what?" I say, voice trembling. "You're not confused; you're scared. You're clearly juggling comfort and illusion, or maybe your pride and ego, hoping nobody calls you out on your bullshit."

"Saliya, here you go with this extra shit…"

"Jameson, you ashamed of me or something? I don't fucking know! But I just ask the bare minimum of your ass. Just a little communication and inclusion, because what you do and don't do really says a lot! It's okay, though." I storm out, and he follows.

"Saliya!"

But I'm down the sidewalk and almost to my car.

"Don't do this, Saliya. You're overreacting!"

I turn around, tears streaming and rage boiling.

"I can't teach you how to be a man or a boyfriend, Jameson! Not while I'm doing the work on myself. I can't do both. Don't call me, don't text me, don't show up at my house on that damn bike trying to 'talk.' You had a lot of time to talk."

I slam my car door, sit in silence for one long minute, and I scream into the steering wheel. I scream until my lungs burn, and then... I drive home.

This isn't a "let it rest" situation. This is a funeral. I've lowered this shit into the ground, covered it with dirt, and walked away without leaving flowers. Jameson Carter can live in the version of love he understands, but I'm not living there with him.

CHAPTER THIRTY-ONE – THE CALL

These days, my dad and I talk more. I don't know what prompted the up in communication, but I'm here for it. I can call him about anything, anytime, and I don't take that for granted.

The older I get, the more I realize my parents are just people; they were doing the best they could with what they had and what they knew. That doesn't erase the ache of the years he chose distance, or she chose pain. The calls he didn't make, the visits he skipped, those memories don't magically disappear.

I see it differently now. No one is perfect, and somewhere in that imperfection, he's still my dad.

It's June 20th and the kids and I are driving home from the mall, bags scattered at the girls' feet, when my phone lights up. The vibration rattles against the dashboard, making me flinch.

My ringer's always off, so the suddenness of it startles me. A California number.

"Hmmm, California? Who the heck could this be...?"

My father, my uncle, my brother, so many roots I don't water enough, live there. My thumb hovers over the screen. I don't know what to expect, but I answer anyway.

"Hello?"

"Hey baby, it's your uncle Brandon. Are you sitting down?"

"I mean, I'm in the car, but let me pull over. Is everything okay?"

"No, baby, it's not okay. Your dad is really sick."

My stomach hollows out like the air has been snatched from me. I grip the gear shift like it's going to absorb what's coming.

"... Sick? What happened? I haven't spoken to him in a couple weeks."

"Well... he stopped breathing, and we don't know why. The hospital's far out; it took too long to get him there. By the time he arrived, he hadn't had oxygen for over four minutes."

"Oh, my God. What?"

My throat closes as I hold my breath, processing the words he's telling me.

"Is he okay? Is he…"

I glance at the girls, my heart breaking as I fight to hold it together, but the dam bursts. Tears stream down before I can stop them.

"Right now he's on life support."

"No…. no. Wait, okay, what are the doctors saying?"

"We're discussing next steps right now. I'll keep you posted, but baby, if you can, please come visit. Come see your dad sooner rather than later. If you can."

When the line goes dead, I crumble. The girls climb into my arms, all soft hands and frantic whispers, trying to piece together what just shattered. But I can't shield them from this.

Within an hour, my ticket's booked for the next week. I use a service through my job since funds are tight, and I have to book an excursion along with it. "Hollywood Hike it is," I say, somber, as I press purchase. It will at least give me the opportunity to decompress while I'm there.

For days, I call the hospital like clockwork, clinging to scraps of updates. Every time, the same flat tone; "no change".

Still on life support, and now there are talks of pulling the machines to test his brain. Each call feels like a countdown, like I'm losing him inch by inch before I even board the plane.

One evening, Uncle Brandon's number flashes again. My body knows before my mind does; my stomach drops to my knees.

"Hello?"

"Hey baby… I don't have good news."

His silence stretches, then shatters.

"The doctors ran the tests. They've said your father has zero evidence of brain activity."

My heart breaks.

"Wait!" It's all I can get out. Words disappear. Air disappears. The sounds all around me grow muffled.

"I'm so sorry," he says, his own voice cracking. "I hate to tell you this. Please still come, Saliya. Be with us, with him. Even if…even if it's just to say goodbye."

The phone slides from my hand. My world folds in on itself. All I can see is every missed birthday, every call he didn't answer. All I can feel is regret for every strength of his I overlooked because I was too busy counting flaws. Not perfect, but still mine. My father.

"Dad." I whisper it into the empty room as Luther Vandross plays in the background, Dance With My Father. It stings. "Dad." I say it louder this time, as if the word itself could keep him.

"Daddy!" I scream until my voice breaks.

"Please, you can't do this to me. Not yet. Daddy, I'm sorry! I don't care how imperfect you are, I just want you back. Please, God, I just want him back! Not right now!"

That night, I fall asleep with his name on my lips, saying it over and over like a prayer.

"Dad. Daddy."

It feels like medicine, like if I say it enough I can keep him close. Then, something strange, like someone walked straight through me. My body seizes, then releases, and I inhale. Peace pours down my spine, soft and heavy. I drift off still whispering his name, clinging to that unexplainable calm.

Friday comes too soon. My suitcase yawns half-open on the floor when my phone rings again. Brandon. My hands shake as I pick up.

"Hey, Unc, what's up?"

"Baby…"

his tone is lighter, almost excited with disbelief.

"Your dad woke up."

I freeze.

"What? No. Unc, don't do this to me. Are you serious?"

I say, trying to make sense of what he's telling me.

"Yes, sweetheart, I promise. This morning he just… woke up! Tried pulling his tubes out. He's not all there yet, not aware of where he is, but he's breathing on his own. He's awake. Your daddy's back. It's a miracle."

Tears rush so fast I'm gasping. "Oh my God, Unc, thank you. Thank you. You don't know; you just made my whole day. My whole life."

By the time I land in California, my nerves are so loud I can barely think. I'm running on fumes, but there's no pause. My uncle is waiting, just as he promised he would be. He grabs my bags, and we go straight from the airport to the hospital.

The air smells like antiseptic and too many endings. My heart hammers until I see him. He's alive. Fragile, but *there*. Relief floods me so hard I almost stumble. I don't get long because the visit wears him out, but it's enough to unclench the fist in my chest.

The next morning, my uncle and his wife leave for work, and the silence in the house presses against me. I get dressed, needing air, needing to move. I walk until I find a little coffee shop tucked under the glow of palm trees.

Behind me, Universal Studios looms like a postcard, while just ahead, people sleep in clusters under the overpass. The contrast hits me in the gut; dreams and harsh reality existing on the same block. I sip my latte and think, *Man, I could live here. It's so beautiful.*

Sunday comes, the day of my Hollywood Sign hike. I lace up my sneakers, adrenaline buzzing under my skin. My Uber drops me at the base; the sun is yawning awake. Four strangers wait with me, but by the time we climb, they don't feel like strangers. We laugh, swap stories about our kids, and when I tell them why I'm here, one woman touches my shoulder and says softly, "I'll keep your father in my prayers." My throat tightens, but I smile.

Step after step, my lungs burn, my legs shake. We stop at lookout points, snapping pictures with the city sprawling wider beneath us. Every turn offers a new outlook on life, a fresh reminder that I'm somewhere I've only ever seen on screens.

And then I'm there. Standing above it all, with the Hollywood Sign just behind me, Los Angeles ahead. The wind whips through my hair, my chest bursting with something bigger than exhaustion, bigger than fear. I lift my face into the sun, warm and blinding, and the words tumble out before I can stop them.

"Thank you, Lord," I whisper into the open sky as I blast Daniel Caesar, Blessed. "Thank you for second chances."

CHAPTER THIRTY-TWO – TORN BETWEEN THE TWO

It's March 2016. Crocheting is my current escape from the noise in my head. The rhythm of the hook and yarn, paired with mindless scrolling on my phone, lets me zone out and breathe. I'm deep into another blanket project I don't need when I hear the familiar ding of a Facebook Messenger notification.

When I glance at the screen, my heart skips. Anthony.

ANTHONY.

I stare at the notification like it might disappear if I blink too fast. It's been years since I've seen or spoken to him. He broke up with me. The hell does this man want.

My mind skips straight to the cringe worthy messages I used to send every few months like clockwork.

Me: You still here?

Me: Hey Anthony, not sure if you use this account anymore, but I'm thinking about you.

Whew. Pure desperation? I cringe so hard my toes curl. "Please tell me he never saw those," I whisper to myself.

Pushing aside my pride, I open Messenger.

Anthony: Good afternoon, Saliya. I know this is unexpected, but I'm going to be in town for a bit, helping my momma out. I would love to see you.

My jaw drops. Anthony. In town. Wanting to see me. Ohhh shit now! I mean, Anthony will always have a soft spot in my heart. Without hesitation, I type back:
Me: Hi Anthony. I would love to see you. Text me so I can have your number.

I hit send, staring at the screen with a mix of excitement and 'girl, don't you dare mess this up' nervousness. The crochet hook goes down. I grab my keys and head straight to Marie's to tell her.

At her kitchen table, I'm picking at the corner of a chipped placemat when I finally say it.

"Anthony texted me."

Marie doesn't even look up from the sweet potatoes she's peeling.

"Anthony who?"

"Anthony. From Norfolk. He's back for a few months," I say hesitantly with a wince.

Her hands freeze mid-slice. Slowly, she looks up.

"Saliya, you can't be serious."

"What? He reached out to me. We're gonna catch up. Harmless?"

Marie drops the peeler like it offended her and crosses her arms. "Harmless? Saliya, what are you doing?"

"Girl, I promise it's not that deep."

She pauses and turns her body towards me.

"See, that's your problem, Saliyaaa. You act like everything's casual until you're knee deep in your damn feelings again, and then I gotta listen to your ass crying about it. Did you forget how badly he hurt you?"

I squirm a little and sit up straighter.

"Damn, Marie! I didn't forget. But people can change. I mean, can't I just pull all the good qualities from every man I've ever dealt with, throw 'em into one body, and have one big great man? Lord, what a prayer." I laugh to lighten the mood.

"Can they change, Saliya?" She says as her eyebrows arch. "Or do you need to believe they can because you don't know how to be alone?"

"Wow, that's not fair," I say, as I feel the heat rising in my face.

"Well, it's the truth, so whatever." She picks the peeler back up but doesn't start working.

"You just had Jameson lying to you. I mean, the man was really stringing you along, and now you want to open the door for Anthony to do the same shit, AGAIN? What exactly are you looking for? Do you even know?"

I press my lips together, because now I feel my attitude on my face.

"I'm trying to enjoy the person in front of me. Whoever that is. I don't want to pick one fucking person right now, is that okay? I need the freedom to figure this shit out, bitch, damn. Peel your potatoes."

Marie slams the peeler onto the counter, the metal clatters.

"Freedom? Girl, this isn't freedom. This is you letting old flames drift back in because it's familiar. They thrive on having access to you, Saliya. Do you think Anthony reached out because he misses you? Or because he knows you'll always answer?"

"You don't get it!" I snap. "You don't know how it feels to wonder if you're ever going to feel something real again, if you missed your person. What if he's my person?"

"I do get it!" she fires back. "And that's exactly why I'm telling you to stop letting these men from your past keep you stuck. You're never going to move forward if you keep looking over your damn shoulder."

I push my chair back from the table. I damn near want to snatch off my earrings.

"Oh, okay, I'm not going to sit here and let you talk to me like this. The fuck is wrong with you today?"

"Then don't," she interrupts me before I can finish my words, "but don't come crying to me when this ends the same way it always does."

I just stare at her for a second, shocked, and grab my purse. Without looking back, I walk out and slam the door harder than I mean to.

Anthony's message has my mind racing all night. By morning, I wake up to his text messages, and before I know it, we spend the day catching up; his momma, his job, a few of his old jokes. We make plans to meet at Fort Monroe, my go-to spot for reflection. Only this time, I'm not here for solitude. I'm here for him.

I'm drumming my fingers on the steering wheel when I spot that familiar white Ford truck pulling up beside me. My heart somersaults.

"Get it together, girl," I say to my reflection. "It's Anthony, and, bitch, we love him."

He steps out, and he brings the damn breeze with him like it's a fairytale. That A-line undershirt clinging to his chest just right.

Lord have mercy on my britches. I'm sorry, Lord, I take that back.

"Hey." I say as I see him walking my way.

"Hey back," he smiles, slow, genuinely happy to see me. "How are you, Saliya? You look...beautiful, baby."

"I'm good. So good to see you." I step closer before I can think twice. My arms and legs are around him in seconds, clinging to him like I've been waiting years for this hug. His arms lock around me, strong and sure.

He teases his words into my temple. "You've missed me, huh?"

"You have no idea."

The next three months feel like stolen time. Weekdays at the gym, evenings with salads and homemade juices, and me re-twisting his locs while our hands linger just a little too long. His momma welcomes me like no time has passed, feeding us like royalty and smiling knowingly.

"You're keeping him happy, aren't you, Saliya?" She says, with her gorgeous white smile.

"I'm doing my best."

I love Anthony's momma so much.

But as summer moves, a bittersweet reality creeps in; his time here is running out.

Anthony's projects are wrapping up, and soon, he'll head back to Georgia.

"Let's spend the day together this Saturday," he says. When I hear it, my heart sinks, but I nod, "Okay. How about pedal boating at the nature park?"

His eyes light up. "It's a date." He seals it with a kiss to my forehead that melts my heart.

Later that night, we tangle up in each other, laying under a throw blanket. Not yet under the bedsheets.

"I really don't want you to go back. But I'm so glad we had this time."

His arms tighten around me.

"Me too, Saliya. You'll always have a piece of me, always."

The pain I feel hurts beyond words because I feel like my person is slipping between my fingers and I can't stop it from happening. "Some days are crazy lonely, Anthony. I don't know what God has in store for me when it comes to love, but I'm okay with His plan. Buttt, I wish you could stay. I love the walks, talks, cuddles, I want all of it."

He smiles faintly as his eyes mist. "Saliya, you should've had my last name a long time ago. I've been lonely too. If I could, I'd walk into every sunset with you. Maybe if I pray hard enough, it'll happen again soon. Until then, I'll be waiting because I love you."

"Thank you for showing me so much about myself," I say, as I try to mask my sadness with happy thoughts.

Anthony laughs. "You think I showed you something? I just held up a mirror. You're beautiful.

But, umm, Saliya, I have to tell you something."

He lifts his head and turns towards me. His eyes are sincere, focused. "You remember when I broke things off years ago?" He's looking me dead in the eye, bracing for the truth to land, and yea, it lands because how the can I forget that shit?

I laugh slowly as I pull my head back and cut my eyes at him. "Yesss, Anthony, I recall. Hard to forget when someone rips your heart out of your chest."

He swallows hard. "Well, I was separated then, and I went back to my wife because... well, she got pregnant. I told myself it was the right thing to do. Noble. Responsible. But it wasn't. It was cowardly."

My pulse is in my ears, and I'm fighting not to get angry all over again. But he continues.

"She didn't think I'd ever file for divorce, thought I'd stay with her forever, unhappy. But I couldn't keep pretending; I should've stayed with you. I've been so miserable, Saliya. I've thought about you every day."

"Okay, so I was really just a side piece? A mistress? Wow, okay, let me make sense of this real quick, Anthony."

"I'm sorry, Saliya, I really am."

"I mean, you must love her, though, right? Because that's a lot of life to give to someone just for it to end like that. Anthony, are you sure you're done?"

"Done, promise, ain't no going back to her."

"Yea, but you said that before, you know? I don't know how to feel about that. I don't know."

He takes my hand. "I'm so sorry. You were the light in my life, and I fucked up. I did. You're one of the good ones, Saliya, the best one."

I stare at our hands. Part of me wants to pull away. Part of me never wants to let go. Years ago, we were both broken. We built each other up piece by piece, only to be torn apart. Now I finally understand why… and the shit hurts all over again.

"Look, you changed my life, and I appreciate your honesty, Anthony." I trace lazy circles on his chest while he plays with my hair.

"You changed mine too. Don't forget that."

The next morning, I force myself to forget about the things said the night before. I just want to enjoy this day. "Aye! It's park day!"

"Hold up, you sound way too excited. Is this about the park or your competitive pedaling skills?"

"Don't start something you can't finish, Anthony."

"Oh, we'll see, baby girl."

A couple hours later on the pedal boats, we climb to an overlook. Fields of flowers stretch in every direction, unapologetically bright. Never Should've Let You Go by Hi-Five plays on Anthony's phone while I'm lost in the view. Anthony slips behind me, arms circling my waist, chin resting on my shoulder. His scent is sunshine and cologne, familiar and intoxicating.

For a moment, I let myself believe we have all the time in the world, but it doesn't hide the pain I feel, knowing that we don't.

"You see that?" he says, lips grazing my ear.

"Hmph, yes, I see. It's beautiful."

"You're beautiful," he says, turning me toward him.

His kiss comes before I can reply; soft at first, then deep enough to feel like a confession, a promise, and a goodbye all at once. And it breaks my heart.

When we get back to the boats and head for the car, the weight of goodbye settles heavy. "I'm not even ready for this," I say.

He takes my hand, his grip warm. "It's not the end, I promise you that, Saliya, always."

"I love you sooooo much, Anthony," I whisper through my tears.

"I love you more," he says, as he wipes them away with his thumb.

"Dry those eyes, gorgeous. You haven't seen the last of me. Always."

I manage a shaky laugh.

"Always, baby."

And then... It's goodbye.

I can't believe he's gone again. I want to believe he's my person. But, God, what is the lesson here. I'm struggling.

CHAPTER THIRTY-THREE – WASH, RINSE, REPEAT

Since Anthony left, I don't know what happened to the woman who used to love the gym. I stopped going. The place reminds me of him, and I'm not built for socializing in a gym, anyway.

My days blur. One folds into the next, momming, working, resting, repeat. Weeks pass in clockwork motion. I'm holding it down, steady, and functional... but the spark is gone.

One fall afternoon in October, on my lunch break, my red-framed glasses are sliding down my nose. My sweater barely hangs on my shoulder, tacos in hand, extra salsa, with a soda to wash it down. My phone rings, and it's a blocked number. I always want to know who's got the nerve to call me with no caller ID.

I answer, and I don't say hello...

"Saliya."

The voice on the other end stops me cold. It sounds...Desperate. I set my food down. "Hello? ...Jameson?" My tone gives away my doubt; I think it's him, but I'm not sure.

"Yes," he says. That's all he says. Oh wow, it is him. The knot in my stomach tightens because I hear the sadness in his tone. "Ummm, Jameson? Hi, what's up?"

"I don't know. I don't even know why I called. I just picked up the phone to see if you still had me blocked."

But his voice doesn't sound right.

"Oh, okay, well no, you're not blocked. But I'm eating right now."

"Damn, you're not gonna ask how I'm doing? My fucking best friend died! You can at least act like you give a fuck about me."

"What? Whoa! Wait. Jameson. How am I supposed to know that? You can't do that! Don't do that to me! Talk to me! Don't call me like this! I'm so sorry. I'm sorry, that's just not something I would know if you don't tell me."

He pauses. I hear sniffles. Something shifts in me, and I hear Marie's voice in my head, *Stop letting these men back in your life*, but I ignore it.

"Okay. Well, I'm on my way to you right now."

I grab my jacket and rush out the door.

Even from miles away, it's insane how I can feel him. The sense of urgency, the sadness.

Jameson and I always had a strong connection… or at least I thought so. We could talk about everything except us. Still, we slip back into an easy rhythm whenever life gets complicated. Comforting him? That's second nature.

It feels a little better this time around, there's more of a light. Dates. Family trips. The connection I'd been waiting for from him.

My favorite moments with Jameson live in the rare spaces where he's vulnerable, when he drops the armor the world taught him he needed. When he laughs hard, shoulders shaking, face lit up, I snap photos and send them to him later. So he can see himself the way I see him: free, unburdened, alive.

He carries so much. I see it in the way his shoulders tense, in the quiet sighs when he thinks no one's looking. So many people lean on him, and even though he says he loves it, I know it's heavy some days. I look beyond his imperfections and love him where he is. Well, I try...

One day, after a week of failed interviews and rejection emails, I'm drained and just want to relax, and so I call him. "Jameson, let's go to the beach and watch the sunset, babe. It's been such a long week and I'm feeling blue."

"Okay, yeah, let me see what the kids want to do."

I can tell he's distracted, but I just want to be around him right now.

We meet at the Icee stand, grab frozen treats, and head to the beach. My mind's heavy with bills, work, and the house I never have time to tend to.

When we arrive, I realize quickly it's a family affair, not us.

I love his people, but today my brain isn't ready to socialize. I want a quiet, intimate moment where I can decompress. Instead, I watch him laughing with his family, playing volleyball, while the wind whips against my skin, alone.

Kids. Bills. Exhaustion. Repeat. I just wasn't ready to be outside like this.

The sun sets on their game as I watch the sunset alone, phone in hand, the light slipping over the water while resentment creeps in. *How can I be in a relationship but still feel so alone?*

"Jameson, I wanted us to have an intimate moment tonight. I really had a rough week and I needed you. Instead, you let me sit alone. I really don't know how to put into words how I feel."

We sit for a second as I watch him process what I just said, and I instantly regret opening my mouth.

"Yo, something's wrong with you. I was right there; you could've said something."

"Jameson, I asked you to go to the beach to watch the sunset. You invited everyone. What else needs to be said? Do I actually need to spoon feed you everything that has to do with being emotionally connected in a relationship? Because I've given you lots of clues and cues, man. This is insane." I throw my keys and purse on the couch and plop down.

"Look, Saliya, you need to get over yourself. Stop being so damn emotional all the time. I'm trying to chill and enjoy my family. You're always doing too much, and you know I'm a family man." But he doesn't understand; it's not about his family at all.

"Listen," I say, calmer now, "we need to talk about how we communicate and interact in this relationship. I'm tired of feeling invisible, and every time I open up, you shut me down like I'm telling you that you did something wrong, I'm helping you understand me, who I am. I don't think you're understanding that. All I need is communication. This isn't a blame game. I just needed…you today."

His eyes flash. "And you wonder why I get like this?" he says. "Every time you open your mouth, you tell me what's wrong with me! I'm still wrong! Look, figure out what's wrong with you, Saliya, because it's not my problem."

"Dude, you're way angrier than you need to be, and I don't have the energy for it."

Loving Jameson is something like opening the fridge and realizing someone ate the last slice of cake you were saving. Oh, and the light bulb is out in the fridge.

Double disappointment. He's just existing in the shallow end of life, I guess. No empathy, no depth, no compassion, no clue. Nothing.

"Jameson, I'm just a soft ass woman who needs some one-on-one time, sometimes. And don't forget to talk to me nice."

"Look, I'm tired of always changing, Saliya. You change to fit me."

Oh boy, just another episode in the Same Shit, Different Day series of Jameson. I quickly end the call, and everything spills out at once: the rejections, the pressure, the loneliness. Then, like Jesus himself said, let's make this day more interesting, my phone rings... again. Another blocked call.

"Hello?" I try to steady myself, but my voice is still raspy and worn from crying and yelling.

"Saliya."

It's the voice I didn't expect but desperately needed to hear.

"Hey, baby girl, it's Anthony."

CHAPTER THIRTY-FOUR – CAN'T LET GO

The flood of warmth and relief hits me like a tidal wave, and I burst into tears.

Lord, what are you doing to me right now? I glance up at the ceiling. "Anthony! Why are you so perfect and always on time?"

My heart is unsure whether to flutter or ache. So I just laugh. We sit in silence for a moment, breathing in the unexpected comfort. "I've had the worst week," I admit, my voice still heavy. "So many rejection emails. It... it gets to you after a while, you know?"

"Well, you know what God has for you is for you, Saliya. So don't stay sad too long. It's their loss, not yours." Without missing a beat, his words land like balm. I exhale, lighter than I've felt all day.

"You're right. Man, I miss you so much. You always know how to make me feel better."

"I wish I could give you a hug, baby girl. Really wish I could," he says, genuine enough to make me believe he'd reach through the phone if he could.

God, I want that.

"Yeah… Anthony, I know. I'm going to relax. Got the next five days off work, so I'm going to make the best of it. Hey, aren't you in Georgia?" Before the thought fully forms, I feel it, the spark. Would I… could I?

"Yup, outside Atlanta. Pull up."

His playful challenge makes me smile through the mess of emotions. "Okay, I'm coming down there. I'll leave in the morning."

I blurt the words out before I can think, and the excitement surges. I love a good challenge. A breath of fresh air. This is happening. What are the odds that this man would call me as soon as I hang up from arguing with Jameson? My goodness.

"Word?" he says, "Don't get my hopes up now, Saliya. Are you for real? I'd love to have you. We'll make sure you relax and have an amazing time. No stress."

Something in me breaks free. The weariness of the past week melts away under the sound of his voice, all that love tucked in his words. Reunited, even if it is just for a moment.

And Jameson? My heart says stop questioning and just have fun. And will!

I can't believe I was just crying over everything wrong, and here's Anthony, not even 30 minutes later. Fate, maybe?

When I wake up the next morning, I don't know how to feel. Nervousness and excitement play a restless tug-of-war with my emotions. The idea of an adventure, and a break from the monotony, sparks a glimmer of hope. And at the end of this road? My man, who's not my man, but could possibly be my man. Yea, I have a problem.

The thought alone keeps my spirits high. The girls are with their daddy, mmm hmm, he's back around, and Georgia is eight hours away. My hybrid is ready; tank full, battery charged, and tires pumped. I have on my stretch pants and a favorite t-shirt for comfort, two energy drinks in the console, and my duffle bag in the trunk.

Pre-dawn is my favorite time to drive; by the time the sun shows, I'll be two hours in with six to go.

I text him: Hey love, I'm starting my drive now.

His reply is instant: Okay, call, and text to keep me updated. Drive safe. I can't wait to see you.

I grin, cheeks aching. He always knows how to soothe the jagged parts of me.

"Okay," I whisper to the empty car.

Playlist on, Junior Mafia's Get Money blasting, I hit the highway. The rush of starting out carries me for a while, but as the miles pass and the wind through the cracked window evens out, so do my thoughts.

Forty is coming. It's not the number; it's everything I thought I'd have figured out by now but don't. Single. Career stagnant. Dreams deferred but still alive. I need this trip, the space to think, to shake loose what's stuck.

Then there's the list of things to do before I turn 40 years old that I scribbled back in January.

Created back when I still believed in fresh starts:

Things to do Before 40
• Beach yoga
• Road trip to see waterfalls in Virginia

- Parasailing
- Mani/Pedi every two weeks
- Horseback riding
- Out-of-country trip for my birthday
- Swimming lessons
- Go fishing
- Write a book
- Thirty-day "I Love You" challenge
- Visit New Orleans
- Random weekend road trip (Check! On my way to you, Anthony!)
- See the sunrise
- See the sunset

The thought of crossing something off feels like a small win.

Four hours in, the horizon stretches wide, now Tupac's Keep Ya Head Up is playing low. Georgia is closer, and Anthony is closer. But I'm not sure if this trip is about him... or about finding myself again. "One mile at a time, Saliya, you'll figure it out."

As I finally pull up to Anthony's house, the fatigue of the road melts away like it was never there. His place looks like something plucked straight from my daydreams, tucked back from the road just enough to feel private, wrapped in towering trees swaying in the late-afternoon breeze.

The greenery isn't just alive; it's art. Flowers in colors so rich they look painted, some I know, some I don't, all whispering of patience and care. The plant lady in me is already scheming. A clipping or two for my collection wouldn't hurt... right?

I ease in behind his white pickup, my pulse ticking up as the front door creaks open. And then there he is, standing in the doorway looking calm and collected, like always. Why is this man so fine? And how am I supposed to walk up to him and pretend my knees aren't plotting against me?

"Aye gorgeous! Glad you made it safely!"

Before I can even get my seat belt off, he's striding toward me, long steps full of confidence and charm. He opens my door with a glacier-melting smile, and I will never get tired of this man's little gestures.

"Yesss, love, I made it, I am so ready to kick my feet up and relax."

He looks at me like I'm worth taking in, from head to toe.

"Hmph, well, let me get your bags and show you to your room; you gotta be tired from all that driving."

He lifts my duffle from the backseat like it's weightless. With him, this kind of care doesn't feel like a favor; it feels necessary. And being with someone who treats it that way is teaching me not to feel guilty about expecting more from love.

Inside, I soak in every detail; the cozy kitchen to the left, the welcoming living room to the right, the way the whole place feels like it exhales peace. Down the hallway, he opens the last door. The room is simple but thoughtful; soft light, a neatly made bed, little touches everywhere that say someone cared enough to think ahead.

"This is where you'll sleep," he says, nodding toward neatly folded towels and a lineup of toiletries arranged like a gift.

"Soap, shampoo, conditioner, lotion, it's all in there. Take your time, get comfortable, and come out when you're ready. I'll be in the living room. Oh, and... when you come out, I got something for you." His voice dips just enough to give me goosebumps.

After he leaves, I linger for a moment, letting it sink in that I'm here and taking in the effort; the intention; the way everything here quietly says I see you and I love you.

In the shower, the smell of something delicious drifts in from the kitchen and makes my stomach growl. I hurry into my favorite sweatpants and an old T-shirt from my aunt; once ankle-length, now skimming my knees, its faded front declaring I Need Coffee.

Cruisin' by Smokey Robinson is playing low as I walk to the kitchen. Then, I miss the small step down into the living room.

"Ohhh my God!" I tumble down the few steps and hit the living room floor. "Well, there goes my dignity. The lord saw another opportunity, I guess."

I burst out laughing and I roll over as if that will somehow help me recover from sheer fucking embarrassment. Anthony rushes over. He smiles as he holds back his laugh.

"Don't you ever change." He says as he hauls me up, and the look on his face makes tripping almost worth it.

I flop onto the couch, cheeks warm from laughter, and prop my feet up. Moments later, he reappears with a plate so perfect it could be on a magazine cover; juicy steak, fluffy rice, bright green beans glisten under the light.

He sits the plate and utensils in front of me. "I knew you'd need a good meal after all that driving. And tomorrow, I thought we could go hiking before the sun gets too hot. What do you think?"

Ugh, this man. He's already got tomorrow mapped out, and not just any plans, but something that speaks to me. Looking at him, I realize it's not just what Anthony does. It's who he is. His gestures are extensions of his heart: big, giving, steady.

I blink fast, trying not to let the tears slip.

"That's perfect. I love you. Thank you for this. For all of it."

"Anytime, Saliya," he says as he leans down to kiss my forehead. We spend the evening binge watch shows and catching up. Eventually, the long drive catches up to me and I fall asleep. Anthony carries me to my bed, and respectfully goes to his room.

The next morning, I wake up to the smell of breakfast, bacon sizzling, sweet maple syrup in the air, Dammit. I can't help the smile that spreads across my face as I roll over.

"This man doesn't quit," I laugh to myself as I hop out of bed.

I get dressed quickly, a pair of black stretch pants, snug camisole, and trusty sneakers. Fanny pack loaded with my phone, no sunscreen because I'm allergic, and I'm ready.

On the table, my breakfast is already waiting. A glass of fresh-squeezed orange juice, a perfect stack of pancakes, bacon, and eggs fluffy enough to make you close your eyes and hum. My heart melts. "Babe, what is this? You're too kind."

Anthony leans against the counter as he packs a small cooler. "You're here to relax, Saliya. No worrying about anything today. Eat. I already had mine. Once you're done, we'll head out. I packed watermelon, cherries, and cold water for the hike."

"You think of everything, don't you?"

"I try. Today's all about you. And trust me, once you see the top of Stone Mountain, you'll never forget it."

The name alone makes me both excited and slightly nervous because I know the history. Still, his quiet confidence fuels me.

At the trailhead, the mountain stands like it's guarding something sacred. Trees frame the path, their leaves dancing in the morning breeze.

Anthony walks ahead with his hand back to catch mine as he plays Stronger by Kanye West.

"You ready for this?"

"I mean, I guess. As ready as I'll ever be. It doesn't look too bad. Just 1 mile up, right?"

I grin, knowing damn well my mouth might write a check that my legs can't cash, but my ass will, if I fall.

The first stretch is easy, shaded, and a gentle incline. But soon, the path tilts up, and the sun burns hotter as my breathing gets heavy.

Oh my goodness, this man is about to have to call the ambulance for me. I'm hands-on-knees within minutes. I look around, and other women are doing the same thing, while the men power ahead like this is nothing. It's humbling... and a little comforting.

I exchange a laugh with the woman next to me. Both of us silently saying, girl, same, with our eyes, Trying to catch our breath. "It's brutal, huh?"

She nods, smirking, "Oh, honey... we ain't even at the hard part yet." A bead of sweat rolls down her temple. "But they say the view's worth it. Guess we'll see," she says.

I glance at Anthony ahead. "Well, if it's not, at least we'll have the stories to tell if we make it out, girl, okay!"

Her laugh is all the encouragement I need to push forward. Anthony slows his pace, waiting for me to catch up. His hand grazes my back as I rest, catching my breath. "You've got this, Saliya. It's tough, but we're almost there. Think about that view."

As we crest the last rise, the world opens up. The view from the top isn't just beautiful; it's breathtaking. Rolling hills stretch into forever, a patchwork of green and brown like it belongs to another world. The cool breeze washes away all of my tiredness. My knees weaken, not from fatigue, but from awe.

"I can't believe this," I whisper.

Anthony's arm slides around my shoulder.

"See? Told you it'd be worth it."

Then, as if on cue, Anthony Hamilton's Best of Me drifts through the air. My heart skips. Anthony grins, extending his arms.

"Dance with me?"

I laugh through the lump in my throat. "Up here? Really?"

"Why not? No better place to celebrate you, a beautiful woman in a beautiful space. Let's dance."

I step into his embrace without hesitation, letting his rhythm guide me. We sway together as the music wraps the moment in magic. My arms curl around his waist; his hands rest easily on my shoulders. Tears sting my eyes, mixed with sweat, as I rest my head against his chest. "I needed this."

He tilts my chin, meeting my gaze. "You deserve this, Saliya. Every single moment of it." We stay like this, suspended between earth and sky, until the song fades. The hike down feels quicker, lighter, full of laughter and teasing. At the car, he hands me a slice of watermelon, and I devour it, juice dripping down my chin.

We sit for a while, flipping through the pictures we snapped on the hike, laughing at how winded I was halfway up.

CHAPTER THIRTY-FIVE – TUMBLED STONE

Back on the road, I stare out the window, heart full. This day is a reminder of what life gives you when you stop fighting and just say yes. Sunlight filters through the trees, turning the car into a warm, quiet cocoon. The silence feels less like emptiness and more like a sanctuary.

"Anthony, have you ever heard of tumbled stone?"

He glances at me, brow raised.

"Tumbled stone? Can't say I have. What is it?" I tuck my legs under me, turning toward him.

"It's stone worn smooth by the elements; water, sand, time. Every curve, every mark tells its own story, ya know?" My voice dips lower. "That's how I feel sometimes… like I've been tumbling for years. Weathered by life. Some days I still feel beautiful, worthy… but some days I'm just plain tired."

Anthony's grip on the wheel tightens, his knuckles grazing my thigh for a fleeting second. "Saliya, you are beautiful. Not despite what you've been through, but because of it. The things that tried to break you, including me, shaped you, and look at you now. Standing strong. Shining! You are light, Saliya. Damn… breathtaking."

I let his words settle between us, heavy in the best way. I didn't expect that from him, but Anthony has a way of sliding beauty into moments I'm not ready for.

"It hasn't been easy. There have been days, hell, years, when I didn't think I could keep going. Like I've been fighting waves on top of waves, and just when I think I can breathe, life pulls me under again. It hurts sometimes. And don't get me started on the single mom life, whew. It can get exhausting, like a hamster on a wheel, you know?"

I stare out the window, reflecting on my life as I talk.

"But even then, Anthony, I still believe in love, in hope. Isn't that crazy?" His hand finds mine, and he rubs my palm softly with his thumb.

"Not crazy, Saliya. It's beautiful. You've been through storms most people couldn't survive, and you are still open, still willing to love. That's not just beautiful, Saliya. That's actually extraordinary."

"You think so?" I say as I turn to him.

"I know so." He says, commanding, like he's telling me I better believe it. "You are enough, you've always been enough, and you WILL always be enough, you hear me?"

My heart swells and cracks at once. "I hear you," I whisper and giggle.

His lips twitch into a smile. "Good. Don't you ever forget it, my beautiful chocolate Nubian Queen."

I laugh, shaking my head. "Oh my goodness, there you go again," I say softly as I laugh, though the lightness feels good.

My eyes close as the music pulls me into the comfort of now. We aren't perfect, but we give each other grace. Space. And for now... it's enough for me.

But when I open my eyes, I'm no longer here. I'm standing at the top of Stone Mountain; the sky stretches wide above me. The air is sharp, electric, the air that warns you something's coming.

Then I see it.

A funnel cloud drops from the heavens, twisting itself into being, dragging the wind into its hunger. The sound rattles the earth beneath my feet as that same Anthony Hamilton song plays in the background, but I don't move.

The tornado howls, and for the first time, since I was nine years old, I howl back.

"Leave us alone, now!!! I'm done running! Leave me alone!"

And then my girls appear at my side, eyes wide with fear. I don't hesitate. I grab their little hands, grip strong.

"Nah, come on y'all, let's go this way! We're not running from this one. We're making it through."

The storm lashes around us, trees bowing low, the mountain trembling, but I keep us moving.

My feet are steady, each step forward defying the pull of the wind. The cellar door is there, right next to Grandma's house; weathered, waiting.

We lunge forward. My fingers grip the handle, and this time, no hands pull me back.

No storm lifts me away. I yank the door open, drag us all inside, and I slam it shut against the roar.

Silence. The silence that feels holy.

I press my back against the cool stone wall, chest heaving, my girls' hands still in mine.

The tornado didn't take me. It didn't take them. It didn't take my voice.

We're safe.

I wake up to Anthony shaking my arm.

"Saliya! Saliya, baby, we're back. We made it to the house. You dreaming hard, girl, damn."

I lean my head back, laughing. Not the nervous laugh of before, but a full, belly-deep laugh that feels like freedom.

"I told you," I whisper, smiling into the dark, "we made it."

It's Monday, September 12, 2017, and the drive back home feels too long, the miles stealing him from me piece by piece. Leaving him isn't the goodbye you cry and scream through; it's quiet pain, almost gentle pain. A silent understanding that we're parting... even if neither of us has said why.

CHAPTER THIRTY-SIX – AWAY FROM THE LIGHT

I want to turn the car around. I want to run back to him, pour out my heart, and tell him all the things I thought I had the courage to say.

As much as it hurts, there's something beautiful about it, something freeing.

I focus on the horizon as the sun dips low, spilling amber and gold across the sky. Each passing mile gives me time to reflect. I don't know what the future holds. One day, if life brings us back together, I'll tell him all the things I couldn't say. Or maybe I won't have to; maybe he'll just know.

For now, I hold on to the gratitude, the laughter, the tenderness, the way he makes me feel like the most beautiful woman in the world. Even if he lied to me, had a wife, got her pregnant and left me to be with her?

Wow, bitch, wow...

I'm interrupted in the middle of my daydream by tires screeching.

A car hits my passenger side. I hear a horn blare, and I see headlights flash as my car smashes into the concrete. Then, silence, except for my panicked gasp before darkness.

I feel suspended in an abyss. Heavy. Floating. A thick, suffocating fog wraps around me, muting everything as I taste the chaos, the danger, the lack of control, unable to speak.

Then the voices begin.

"...machines are stable... give it time..."

"...still no response?"

"...be patient... she's strong..."

I want to scream, *I'm here!* I want to fight my way out. But the darkness keeps pulling. Then, like a flicker in the black, I hear her. My momma's voice, trembling.
"Saliya... wake up for me..."
Then I hear Marie's muffled sniffles.

"Momma?" My mind screams it, but my body won't obey. Something foreign presses in my throat, choking the sound. My eyes flutter open against the harsh glare of hospital lights.

"Oh, my girl!" Momma cries. "Doctor! My baby woke up!"

Marie's hands fly to her mouth. "Oh my God, Saliya..."

My coughing interrupts her as the nurse pulls the tube, and my throat is painfully raw. "What... happened?" I try to speak through my raspy, sore throat.

"Just relax; you were in a terrible accident." Momma says as she rubs my head to comfort me. "In Virginia Beach, Saliya. You broke a couple of ribs, your leg... you hit your head so hard they had to put you in a coma to control the swelling. An entire week!"

"Momma, a week? What's today's date? Where are the girls?" Before I can process what she's saying, there's a knock on the door. A low, almost hesitant voice:
"Um... hello, is it okay to come in? It's Jameson." Every nerve in my body tightens. I can't tell if it's relief or dread.

"Yes," I rasp.

Momma glances at Marie. "Come on, let's get some food. They need to talk." The door clicks shut behind them, and Jameson steps forward. Even in the harsh hospital lighting, his tall frame looks... smaller. His eyes are red and swollen.

"Saliya, God, I thought I'd lost you."

I force a smile I don't feel. "Thanks... for being here."

"Your mom called me. I've been here every day. Praying. Look, this may be crazy, right, but I don't want to waste another second, Saliya. Not one."

I roll my eyes. *Momma.* Before I can ask what he means, he drops to one knee, nearly tangling himself in the IV lines. "Jameson...wait."

He looks up at me, "Let me finish," he interrupts.

"Saliya, this week reminded me of everything I'm too stubborn to admit. I love you; I need you, and I want to build a life with you ..." He reaches into his pocket, pulling out a small velvet box.

"Will you marry me?"

Time freezes as my eyes dart between him and the ring, images at the top of Stone Mountain with Anthony float in my head.

"Jameson...I..." The words are caught in my throat.

"We're really not compatible, Jameson." I can hardly see through my tears and my head swims with emotions too complex to name. I think my damn blood pressure just went up.

"Say yes," he pleads, "I can't lose you, Saliya. I'm gonna work on everything we talked about before. I promise. Just say yes."

"Yes, Jameson. I'll marry you." Relief floods his face as he slips the ring onto my finger, and I believe our second chance, or third, or fourth. Whatever. It's our moment! But even as my momma and Marie burst in, shouting with joy, a voice in my head whispers: *Do you trust that he's different this time?*

Later, when the room empties and the quiet settles in, I stare at the ring, letting the diamond catch the light like it's trying to blind me into certainty.
"I'm engaged."

Talking to myself, testing the words. They taste strange. Am I happy? A soft knock pulls me from my thoughts. The door creaks open, and I see locs first.

"Anthony…"

His face is straight, his jaw tight. "Saliya, My mom called me. She told me about the accident, and I came straight here the next day."

Guilt floods me instantly. "Thank you… Anthony, for coming."

His gaze drops to my hand. "Is that… a ring?"

"Anthony, I—"

"Jameson?" He cuts me off, visibly angry. "You're engaged? To him?"

"I… I didn't know what else to do. He asked me, and I felt like it's what I wanted at that moment."

"You didn't know what else to do?" His words mixed with laughter come across bitter. "What about us, Saliya? That didn't mean anything? We were together; we just had sex LAST WEEK! Now you're engaged!"

I reach for him, but he steps back, just far enough that I can't touch him. "Anthony, please… I'm sorry, I—"

His eyes harden. "You're not sorry. You made a choice. And do you know what? That's fine." His voice drops. "But don't you fucking act like I didn't matter. Don't you rewrite what we had to make this make sense for you just so you don't feel bad about what YOU just did to me."

For a second, I think he's going to soften up a little, but then he looks at me like he's memorizing my face for the last time. "You could've been honest with me; you didn't have to love me halfway; you could've been honest...with ME, Saliya!"

He turns for the door, and I can't find my voice fast enough. "Anthony!" He stops with his hand on the handle, shoulders stiff, but he doesn't look back.

"I get it now. And trust me, you'll get it too, when you realize the difference between being chosen... and being cherished. That man don't fucking want you." The door closes behind him.

I gasp for air, and the ring on my finger suddenly feels like a cuff. He's gone, and I'm just wondering what prank reality show I'm on because this just can't be life. I just got a tube out my throat, got engaged, and got cussed out all at once. Shit!

CHAPTER THIRTY-SEVEN – SO LONG AS YOU ARE FREE

The day finally arrives, April 3, 2018. The morning sun beams gently through the lace curtains, casting warm light onto my skin as I stand in the mirror. My wedding dress is a vision of elegance; a work of art draped in shimmering ivory satin. It hugs my body with precision, highlighting every curve before cascading into a dramatic train that pools around my feet like a silken river.

The back of the gown is exquisitely bare, showing the smooth curve of my spine and the strength I carry underneath. I love a good backless moment. The plunging V neckline is delicately lined with intricate beadwork that sparkles like morning dew. Long sleeves grace my arms with the same embellishments, each stitch catching the light.

My hair is in a soft, regal loc up-do; a crown of pipe curls, interwoven and sculpted to perfection. A delicate veil floats behind me, pinned seamlessly into the up-do and trailing down the train, a whisper of grace and finality.

I stare at my reflection, at the soft locs framing my face, the glow of my skin, the eyes that have survived storms and still found a way to shine. This is my moment, our moment. It wasn't born from fairy-tale love, but from resilience. Here we go.

As I step into the aisle, a familiar melody slips into the air. Anthony Hamilton's Best of Me is playing.

I whisper to myself as my smile drops for half a second. "The fuck?" I feel sick to my stomach, but I keep walking. I hear Anthony's laugh in my head, the way he teased me about my hiking shoes.

"What am I doing?" I say as I force a smile. The camera phones click and flashes pop. "It's the happiest day of my life," I repeat the words under the veil like a mantra, willing myself to believe it.

Then I see him.

Jameson is standing at the altar, tall, grounded, and breathtaking in a tuxedo that looks like it was born for him. Deep black, perfectly tailored, satin peak lapels, crisp white shirt, black bow tie, every detail precise. His freshly shaved head gleams under the lights; his goatee is sharp enough to cut glass. His cufflinks glint, his pocket square sits perfectly folded, and his polished shoes reflect the church lights like tiny mirrors.

And those eyes... steady, deep brown, locked on mine. They've been my anchor more than once, but am I ready for this?

The music fades, and my steps bring me closer, and yet... I can't shake this damn feeling. I'm terrified. My smile stays, but something in me stirs, a restless whisper that this day feels more like a performance than a beginning.

The pastor clears his throat.

The faint creak of the church doors interrupts my thoughts, but I keep looking at Jameson.

"SALIYA!"

The voice doesn't just enter the room; it rips through it, making every head whip toward the back. I stumble, and my pulse spikes.

I squint, blinking against the sunlight pouring through the doorway, but I know the voice before I see the face. That voice is carved into me like scripture.

"Anthony?"

I breathe, eyes still locked on Jameson, barely moving my lips.

Jameson's grip on my hand tightens so much that it hurts, and I yank my hand away. "Jameson, ouch! My goodness!"

His jaw ticks once, his look towards me darkens, then cuts to the back of the church. Rage flashes across his face, and then disbelief, then something that looks like fear. His nostrils flare, and his shoulders stiffen like he's ready to swing at someone, right here in front of God and everybody.

Please don't let them fight in front of Jesus.

Anthony steps forward just enough to be seen, the sunlight from the stained-glass windows catching his face. Those eyes, stormy, desperate, and unwavering.

"You know this isn't what you want!"

Gasps ripple through the crowd like a wave. Someone's phone drops to the floor with a clatter. My mother's hand flies to her mouth.

I can hear my heartbeat in my ears, over everything else, pounding, screaming.

Jameson's hand clamps down on mine again, not a lover's grip anymore but a shackle. His voice is low, lethal, a growl that only I can hear. He's pissed.

"Don't you even think about it, Saliya, don't."

His knuckles are white. His eyes, usually warm, are like shards of glass. No, he's not just pissed; he's humiliated, his pride unraveling with every second Anthony stands there.

And then Anthony delivers the blow.

"You know we're supposed to be together. I love you, Saliya, and you love me!"

My heart sinks to my ass in that moment.

"Lord, have mercy," a woman mutters as the church erupts in gasps and whispers.

Marie's eyes are wide as saucers, and she mouths, *what the fuck?*

My aunt shakes her head so hard her hat tilts sideways.

Our family's faces are a gallery of outrage and disbelief, each expression sharper than the last.

But none cut deeper than Jameson's. He doesn't look like the man waiting to marry me anymore. He looks like a man betrayed in front of his family, fists clenching at his side, holding himself back from storming the aisle. His chest heaves, his throat working like he's choking on words he can't force out.

I try to move, but my feet feel cemented to the aisle. "Anthony…" I whisper. Jameson turns toward me, disbelief flashing in his eyes. Saying his name out loud feels like a knife to him. His jaw drops, but no sound comes. Just raw devastation caught in his throat.

"I can't," I say, staring at the floor, tears burning my eyes, but Anthony doesn't flinch. His stare pins me in place.

"Look at me, Saliya!" Anthony takes a step forward. And then another. "Look me in the eye and tell me you don't love me. Say it, Saliya, and I'll walk out right now. I swear to God I'll never bother you again."

Everything around me is moving in slow motion. The preacher has his hands raised, trying to calm the room. My cousins are whispering too loudly, feeding the storm. My mother cries, and shame crumples her face.

And Jameson, his hand drops from mine, fingers curling into a fist at his side. His eyes plead with me, *choose me. Please choose me.*

I'm borderline hyperventilating because I want to be anywhere but here. And then I move, no, I run.

My dress lashes against my legs, the silk train snapping like an angry wave as I tear down the aisle. Gasps turn into shouts, the scrape of my heels echoing off the wooden floor. The room is chaotic now, a hundred jumbled questions chasing me to the side door.

Behind me, I hear Jameson's voice, "Saliya, don't walk out that door!" But I don't look back. I can't.

By the time I burst outside, the cool air smacks me like a slap I didn't see coming. My lungs are burning; my legs are threatening mutiny.

Anthony's voice is losing strength as he rounds the corner just as I stumble onto the sidewalk. His hands find my waist, steadying me before I can hit the ground. I collapse against him, clutching his shirt.

"Anthony..." The sob rips out of me before I can stop it, my words muffled against his chest. "I love you, I'm so sorry, I'm so, so sorry."

He holds me tighter, burying his face in my hair. "I couldn't let you go, Saliya. I couldn't."

I can barely breathe as he grabs my face. His eyes search mine like he's trying to find the girl he once knew.

"Come with me, come on. Let's go. Get the kids, leave the rest behind. It's you and me."

I nod through my tears and scoop up the heavy train of my dress; the fabric dragging behind me like the last thread of the life I'm leaving. Anthony guides me to his car. I don't have my phone, bouquet, or even my thoughts in order, just this gown, and Anthony at my side.

We slide into the seats, both of us out of breath. He glances at me, then reaches over, lifting my veil, his thumb brushing away a tear.

"I couldn't let you marry him," he says. "I couldn't let you make the biggest mistake of your life."

Right on cue, a car zooms past, blasting Pharell's song, Happy.

I tilt my head back toward the roof of the car, like it's the sky, staring sarcastically at God. Then I look at Anthony, feeling my world shift without my permission.

"Anthony, I'm not leaving with you. I'm just... leaving. I can't do this anymore. With either of you."

I love you so much, but what's done is done. You didn't choose me; you came back around for me when you realized you weren't happy. And Jameson only came back because I almost died! I don't deserve any of this confusion. I don't. Neither of one you really even chose ME!"

I slowly pull away and watch his hand drop to his lap. Then I open the door and step outside the car. The click of the door closing feels so good to my soul.

Anthony hesitates but then hits the gas. The engine roars, and he's gone. Gone from the church, from the future we silently promised each other, from the idea that love alone could fix what's broken.

I stand there until the taillights fade into nothing, then turn toward the church doors just as people spill out, their faces full of questions I'll never answer.

My dress wraps around my legs, the satin catching at my knees as I kick off my shoes and take off running again. The cool ground bites at my bare feet, but I don't stop. I steal one last glance at the steeple, shrinking with every step, and draw in a deep breath.

I don't know where I'm headed. I know my heart is torn between mourning a love I wish could suffice and seeking freedom. But one thing's certain: I choose me this time. I keep running until the church disappears behind me and a bench finally comes into view.

"Oh my goodness, let me sit down."

I rip the veil off my head, ripping it off my life too, and toss it in the trash. People stare, but honestly? I'd stare too if I saw a barefoot woman in a wedding dress, gasping for air, throwing away her veil with no bridal party in sight.

When my breathing slows, I stand, and I smile. And it's a real, genuine smile. "I'll send out cards next week. I'm tired." Then, I walk away from everyone.

Anthony and I never speak again. My heart breaks a little, but it's a clean break; the kind that heals straight.

Jameson reached out once, told me I broke his heart. And he's right, I hurt him. I hurt him by coming back when I should've stayed gone, by loving him harder than I loved myself, by trying to build depth in shallow water.

I finally understand that I had to wipe the slate of my past clean to grow into the woman I was meant to be. Maybe Marie was right.

Sometimes peace isn't about fixing what's broken, it's about finally putting the pieces down because it's broken beyond repair.

EPILOGUE

Three years later, it's September 2021, and life has truly blessed me. The air is cooler now, with that crisp fall breeze that carries both endings and beginnings, and I reflect on just how far we've come.

Heaven, now 15, attends art classes part-time. She keeps her sketchbook with her everywhere she goes, doodling on the bus, shading during family movie night, leaving soft graphite fingerprints across the kitchen table I can never quite scrub away.

Nicole, 17, is preparing for college after graduating early. She walks around the house with pamphlets and course catalogs spread out like puzzle pieces, dreaming out loud about majors and dorm rooms and whether she'll need a mini-fridge.

Christina, my 14-year-old, is finally healthy after months of uncertainty. Her digestive issues that once kept me awake at night, pacing hospital halls and praying for answers, are now only a memory. The allergist fixed what no one else could, and these days her laughter is louder than her pain ever was. We're all blossoming in a space created by honesty, hard conversations, and learning not to run from truth.

Marcus is still, well, Marcus. I ran into one of his ex-girlfriends not too long ago, and she said that he tells people he left me because I cheated. Cheated? Yes, that part is true. But left me? No, sir. Let's not rewrite history. He also says he put me through college, which is another lie told with a straight face. What he put me through was debt.

Debts I had to crawl out from under, debts tied to apartments and utility bills I never signed for, even a bank account that sat in the red more than $2,000 because of his lies. There was even a federal investigator looking for him because he refused to return a rental car, drove it like it belonged to him, like consequences didn't apply. But those are his truths to carry. Mine is different: gratitude for better choices, and the freedom to start over clean.

I chipped away at my "Before I turn 40" list of things to do, each item like a candle lit for myself. It took longer, but I did it! I took a solo hiking trip and discovered that silence on the trail can feel like prayer. I went parasailing, letting the wind hold me when I didn't fully trust it would. I rode horseback through open fields and felt small in the best way, reminding me life is bigger than my pain.

And then there is my small business, my little shop of crocheted blankets and scarves. It started slowly, imperfectly, with more tangled yarn than finished projects, but joy stitched itself into every piece. I watched it grow roots, spreading from local markets to online orders, until one day I realized the business was no longer just about sales. It was about proof. Proof that I could create something sustainable, something warm, something that is mine.

One by one, goal by goal, I honored my promises to myself. The real victory wasn't in checking the boxes, but in realizing that I am capable, resilient, and worthy of every damn dream I once thought was too fragile to say out loud. Life isn't perfect; it's mine. And that is more than enough.

Today, as I close the store, the sun dips behind the buildings, and a gust of wind whips through, sending leaves swirling in every direction. The leaves fly right into my face, blinding me for a second, and in the middle of that flurry, my basket of yarn slips. Skeins tumble across the sidewalk like wild things trying to escape me.

I laugh under my breath, entertained at myself as I chase a stubborn skein that's rolling toward the street.

"Oh, let me help you." A deep baritone voice catches me off guard, snatching my focus instantly. I turn and see a man kneeling across from me, already scooping up yarn without hesitation. His hand shoots out. "Hi, I'm Joshua. Let me, uh…help you up?"

For a moment, I hesitate. But something in his eyes gives me pause, no push, no performance, just patience and sincerity. I exhale, and my fingers slip into his as he pulls me gently to my feet. He smiles, holding out the last ball of yarn.

"You look like you can use a third arm," he says.

I laugh, "Or maybe I need a basket with a lid."

"Or…you need someone who doesn't mind carrying it for you. Wow, you are beautiful. I especially love this beauty mark. Would I be too forward if I asked you to tell me the story behind that one day?"

"I would love to tell you all about it one day, Joshua."

Love without self-worth or direction isn't love; it's hunger. And that desperate hunger will eat everything in its path, destroying it. I know that now. And as Joshua's hand lingers just a second longer in mine, I realize wholeness doesn't mean walking alone. It means knowing that I can and choosing when I don't have to. I used to think beauty was what came after the pain. Now I know, beauty is what survived it. My thorns make my roses beautiful, and this is my story.

"Siri, play Cardi B, Get Up 10!"

AFTERWORD – THE GIRL WHO WROTE THROUGH THE STORM

These are the words of the girl I used to be, the one who survived what she couldn't yet name, and wrote her way through the silence. Before I became her; the woman who healed, I was her; the girl who endured. These poems were written between 9th and 12th grade, before I had language for trauma, before I knew what healing looked like. I didn't realize it then, but every line was a lifeline. Writing became my way of surviving, of telling the truth before I could say it out loud. These are her words; unpolished, emotional, honest, exactly how she wrote them.

A Smile Not Yet a Smile

Mumbling words my mouth and heart could not yet decipher.

Remembering images from a love not able to pull apart.

Abuse from physical to emotional, will I ever come to understand the strange connection?

Breath taken, tightly gripping the last bit of pride left deep in my soul.

Hearing the sounds of a heart scorned, its cries hurt my ears so, A sound I can't ignore.

Why is it that a smile can hurt the heart more than a cry? I hurt myself with that question.

It is a smile not yet a smile.

Hiding pain that hurts to the highest extent.

A child unable to cope with the stresses of adult life.

Rage building up so much anger that to release it all at once would be a crime.

A cause not able to point out,

I don't want to cry any longer, don't even want to laugh any longer.

It seems like when I feel I'm getting stronger;
you break me down and then I start to hurt.

You remind me what I'm not worth.

I don't want to let anyone else in, yet I don't want
to let this love out,

I think my street has come to an end, but is it too
late to just turn around?

Too much harm has been done, too many
feelings settled in.

To get where I need to be, I'll just have to lose a
couple of friends.

I have yet to strengthen my smile that is not yet a
smile.

<u>You Stole It, but I Gave It Away</u>

I always loved roses, but you made me hate
flowers.

You stole it, but I gave it away.

I always yearned for closeness, but you only
manipulated me with your power.

After certain moments, you can never be the
same.

I always wanted someone to talk to, but your
words cut like a knife,

I always said I would be quick to forgive in my
pain,

But your eyes soothed the pain of the scars like
Novocain.

A glimpse of my future and all I see is rain.

So naïve, I believed you wanted something
more,

But once you got what you wanted, you were out
the door.

You called me out of my name, but hey, I'm used
to that.

Model of dysfunction that, with its absence, I
would've never looked back.

I will never look back because you stole it, but I gave it away.

Now I'm sitting here crying because I know I'll never be the same.

<u>Fantasy</u>

Can I just stay here in this corner as the world
passes me by?

Can I just not cry?

One, two, three, four, five, six...the seconds move
so slow.

Just me and him, just me and him, I'll just let it all
go.

I'll just take a step forward, what could be so
hard.

Fall right into it and try not to look ahead too far.

Yes he loves me, yes he loves me and not
perfection.

Yes he loves the way I move, loves the attention.

Why can't I just stay here in this corner as the
world passes me by?

Why can't I just not cry?

So hesitant...

Seven, eight, nine, ten, eleven, twelve...the hours
make my heart race.

Just us alone, Just us alone, between me
and him I will reduce the space.

I will just close my eyes, step forward and it will
be so good.

Take this moment and I will cherish it, back I will
not look.

Yes this is happening, yes it's now and maybe not
forever.

Yea he loves the way I love, the way our bodies
feel together.

It was heaven as I counted...

One, two, three, four, five, six, seven, eight, nine,
ten, eleven, twelve.

As my fantasy winds down...

And here I sit, still in this corner as the world
passes me by.

I will just choose not to cry.

Because a fantasy was all I wanted,
but what I now have is you and me.

My fantasy...

Missing You

How can one get through a moment in time missing the one piece that completes them?

If you know please tell because the days get harder and harder without you.

Never knowing love like this love but knowing one thing will forever remain.

A love that still stands strong, or infatuation?

Either way, my dreams are still filled with images that help me through this hard time.

I will get through.

A love so rare, so hard to find, a love that just silences the world.

Leaves but one path leading to but destiny.

You and me.

For you love I will wait an eternity.

If only in the end I am left with the greatest gift of them all,

You.

No gift could compare to your love so sweet.

Until I am wrapped in your arms once more, I am... Missing you.

Lost Love

Unusual desire,

Bringing coldness to my heart as I watch you.

Your ever-changing presence.

Standing with displeasure.

How many steps must I take for you to notice me?

Winter smothers me as the up drafts blow around sounds of laughter, very heartfelt.

I struggle to escape this ocean of jealousy that kills me slowly but surely.

How long will this last?

A stare that can melt hearts, I do resist not.

Oh, at night regrets do fill up my head, every portion of my mind.

One day, just maybe, this wish will fall back on me.

Right now, though, I am sending it back up to the stars in the sky.

As the winds cut across my face, I fall into a dream of being forever lonely.

There is only one in which I would like to hold me.

The stare of my eyes is so strong, for I see your indelicate actions.

But of that you know nothing.

How loud must I yell for you to hear the cries of my love, my love?

For now, my voice is slowly fading and is not but a whisper.

For what I yearn you will, then, never come to find.

Many Times

Funny the many times I have passed this building, never has it caught my eye.

Never so beautiful and tall had it stood, never so soft had been the color.

So hypnotizing was the shadow, as if calling your destiny and your fate.

On my way though, I must go.

Funny the many nights looking at this moon so full,

Never had it shone so bright.

Never so meaningful has been such an inanimate object.

As though spelling out a name, as if crying

Just stop, cherish this moment.

But still on my way, now, I must go.

Funny the many times into someone's eyes I have looked,

Yet never have I once become lost.

Never so speechless had I been or rare a moment placed upon me.

Never so profound a feeling of relief,

So brief a moment has left a print in my heart.

As though reassuring, worry no and fear not

Still, on my way I must go.

Funny the many times I've fallen, never has a fall been so sweet.

Never so significant has been a timing, so beautiful an artless place.

Very fascinating was the figure, a familiar touch, harmless and true.

I have fallen in love…

If Tomorrow Were to Never Come

If tomorrow were to never come, I haven't said all I wanted to say.

I haven't told you I loved you enough, I didn't give you one last hug.

If tomorrow were to never come.

If today were my last, I wouldn't be satisfied with all that I did.

I wouldn't have learned from all my little mistakes.

I would have many regrets.

Fade…

As you do so slowly in and out of my life now.

I try to live as if there were not tomorrow, but what if…

If it were to never come, would you love me like you used to?

Would you hold me, run your fingers through my hair like you used to?

When we never thought about tomorrow, just now.

You and me.

If tomorrow were to never come,

Would I think about the phone that seldom rings now with you on the other end?

It's all my fault, but...

Would I want to hear your voice tonight, this one night?

So still...

If tomorrow were to never come, no matter how I have questioned this friendship,

If this were my last day, know that I love you.

ACKNOWLEDGMENTS

To my mother, thank you for being strong in the moments when you needed softness, and soft in the moments when strength would've broken you. You taught me balance way before I had language for it.

To my father, thank you for showing me that forgiveness doesn't mean forgetting, and that someone almost dying doesn't erase their bad habits. You taught me to forgive with my eyes wide open and to understand that some people never change.

To my good, good girlfriends; y'all kept my sane on more days than you'll ever know, each relationship perfectly placed in my life. You pulled me back from absolute destruction even when it was never your responsibility. You loved me through the versions of myself I was still trying to grow out of. Thank you.

To Apostle Jackson and First Lady Chiara Jackson; thank you for reintroducing me to God, grace, and mercy in a way that finally landed. I grew up in church, but something at Salt of the Earth Ministries in Oklahoma Shifted me for the better. (And Lord, I hope they never read this book and make it to this page.)

To every liar, manipulator, and cheater; SURPRISE! You're probably in here with a different name. Thank you for the lessons, the character development, and the plot twists. Whew! I finally understand what all of that pain and confusion was preparing me for.

And last but absolutely not least: If I was ever the villain in your life, in your story, I want you to stop, take a breath, and ask yourself...

"What in the fuck did I do to piss her off?"

About the Author

Saliya Rose wrote *Before It's Beautiful* as an act of truth-telling and self-preservation. This story was not written to explain pain, but to honor survival and the moments that shaped it. It is a record of what was endured and what was learned along the way. She hopes readers find recognition rather than instruction within these pages.

Sometimes, you have to be okay with being the villain in someone else's story.

Saliya lives in Virginia with her four daughters.

www.ingramcontent.com/pod-product-compliance
Lightning Source LLC
Chambersburg PA
CBHW031116160726
47991CB00004B/1417